DEAD

A CELEBRATION
OF MORTALITY

CHARLES SAATCHI

THE
RUSSIAN
MAFIA KNOW
HOW TO GIVE
YOU A NICE GRAVE.

HERE, AT THE SHIROKORECHENSKOYE Cemetery, stand the gravestones of some of the most ruthless gangsters in Russian history.

The industrial city of Yekaterinburg, located in the vast frozen landscape of the Ural Mountains, was torn apart by warring members of the gangs in the 1990s, and continues to be dogged by their activities today.

Each intricately carved tombstone depicts a portrait of the man whose grave it marks.

Most are bedecked in well-cut suits, with slick haircuts and serious jewellery – a mark of the wealth that a life of crime

DEAD

was able to afford the gang members – albeit a precarious one.

Some are pictured alongside something they greatly loved; a Mercedes Benz, a BMW, food and wine, or simply a clenched fist.

Detailed in their verisimilitude, the stones stand as a testament to the level of menace the gang member achieved in life, and the duration of the respect they command beyond life.

The cost of a memorial is no less eloquent than the image adorning it; many cost upwards of £20,000.

The tombs today have a bizarre second life as a tourist attraction for the city.

Intrepid visitors have to negotiate frequent muggings and intimidation by remaining gang members, who stake out the graveyards to protect their boss's final resting place.

Very often their leaders are buried with gold, and tombs have been known to be raided.

These appealing tombstones are common to cemeteries across cities in Russia, Ukraine, Armenia, Belarus, and Georgia.

What unites each of the men buried beneath is their status as 'thieves-in-law', official criminals who abide by a strict code of behaviour.

This class of gangster appeared in the gulags of the Soviet Union as a set of men who refused in any way to adhere to the demands of their prison warders or indeed the state.

There are now estimated to be 300,000 gang members in Russia and affiliated internationally, operating on local and governmental levels, making it one of the most extensive and powerful in the world.

The success of the mob across Russia is mirrored in the management of the nation.

In 2008 Wikileaks released a U.S. report on the state of Russian politics and concluded that much of the country was

DEAD

being run as an autocratic kleptocracy, or a virtual 'mafia-state'.

Bribery was rife with estimates placing the amount of money exchanged in Russia for the purposes of pay-offs at $300 billion.

Arms trafficking, money laundering, protection for gangsters and their offshore accounts are allegedly commonplace activities at various levels of government.

It is then perhaps no surprise that the Uralmash 'family', whom these particular tombs commemorate, have extended their activities into the political realm.

The Uralmash gang was the most powerful in Yekaterinburg, Russia's fourth largest city.

Since the dissolution of the Soviet state they seized control of local business, working up from kiosks at petrol stations to the Uralmash power station, growing their empire through coercion and protection rackets.

They eventually commanded a higher income as an organisation than the city itself.

Putin's appointment as President saw a decline in violent crimes and an end to the height of mafia power in the area.

However in 2008 reports of assassinations were on the rise once more, hardly surprising given 30% of the area's vast economy was in gangster hands.

The Uralmash gang's ascent to power was not a smooth one, and major clashes with other mobsters took place throughout the 1990s in what were locally known as the Mafia Wars.

At the time it was not uncommon for residents of the city to hear explosions nearby as the Uralmash clashed with the Blues and Centrals, using grenades, rocket launchers and machine guns.

Comprised mostly of long-hardened teams of thugs controlled by the Tsyganov brothers, the gang was also driven at the time by internal conflict.

A new brigade of younger men was keen to seize power from the founding members.

This rebellion was brutally quelled, with the old guard ruthlessly cracking down on the would-be gang leaders.

The gang is bizarrely involved in public life in the area, beyond the bribing of politicians that one might predict.

In the 1990s they set up a vigilante group called 'City Without Drugs'.

After the demise of the Soviet Union the borders were opened to Asia and surrounding nations with an accompanying surge in prostitution, black market goods, and drugs.

The city of Yekaterinburg suffered particularly from an influx of heroin, and the Uralmash took it upon themselves to rid the city of the scourge.

Whether this was in order to improve their 'status' or retain control of its criminal underworld is much debated.

Led by gang members, citizens of the city would roam the streets looking for drug addicts and dealers.

When a dealer was caught he would be beaten senseless, and his home burnt down.

One dealer was found tortured savagely and tied to a tree with a sign around his neck stating that he was poisoning local children.

Addicts were brought to the gang's newly founded drug treatment centre; they would be fed bread and water, hand-cuffed to a bed or radiator, and forced to go cold turkey.

The police, probably sympathetic with the group's activities, did nothing to intervene, stating that no-one had come forward to make an official complaint.

This public relations success for the gang bolstered their on-going campaign to gain power in local politics.

They legitimised their business interests, becoming legal controllers of much of the local industry, and registered themselves as a political party – the Social-Political Union Uralmash.

Murderer had become politician in one fluid movement, organising 'The Day of the Child' events rather than vicious bank raids.

Gang members would work without pay in schools as guards, ensuring the kids were well behaved and not smoking.

They delivered food parcels to old-aged pensioners, and even television sets.

Not surprisingly, in 1998 their candidate Alexander Khabarov was elected into the state government.

NOBODY KILLED WARLORD ATTILA THE HUN.
HE DIED OF A NOSEBLEED.

AT HIS WEDDING PARTY IN 453 AD TO HIDILCO, a Germanic princess and the latest of many wives, Attila's nose started bleeding.

He was too drunk to notice, and he drowned in his own blood, discovered dead the next morning.

Attila had ruled the Hunnic Empire for the last thirteen years; in the early days of his reign he shared power with his brother Bleda, but decided it would be more congenial if he arranged for his brother to be murdered.

The Roman historian Priscus reported that Attila was highly intelligent, and extremely modest in his clothing.

He described him as short in stature, but with an exceptionally broad chest, and large head. His eyes were small, his beard thin, he had a flat nose and deeply tanned skin.

Priscus warned the Roman senate early, in the first year of Attila's triumphs, that he would become a formidable enemy, burning with a fervent rage, and determined to gain control of many of Rome's Germanic neighbours.

Attila had built a mighty war machine, and unleashed it on

the major cities of the Balkans, beating Rome's top Imperial Legions twice in open battle.

In fact, although his period of Hunnic power finally resulted in the creation of Hungary, his real interest was in accumulating great wealth.

The booty he gathered from defeated cities was vastly increased by his extortion scheme, whereby he agreed to leave potential targets alone if they paid enough ransom.

He collected 2,000lbs of gold each year from Constantinople, and probably a larger sum from the senate, who had asked Pope Leo I to persuade him it would be more profitable not to attempt to sack Rome.

To all he vanquished, he was known as the Scourge of God.

Rome watched in horror as he expanded his grip throughout Austria and Germany, plundering and devastating all in his path.

They were forced to pay his bounty after he overpowered the Italian city of Aquileia and the Lombardy region.

The town of Venice was created when the residents of nearby areas fled there, as they were being ravaged by Hun armies.

His triumph as the world's most ferocious leader was only eclipsed in the 13th century by Genghis Khan, ruler of the Mongol Empire that united the nomadic tribes of northeast Asia.

His control encompassed all of China, Korea, the Caucasus nations, and substantial portions of Eastern Europe, Russia, and the Middle East, the largest contiguous empire in history.

He, too, relied upon his reputation for ferocity to achieve and maintain his grip, with most territories simply caving in when his forward troops made an appearance on their borders.

Historians cannot agree about Genghis Khan's death, and theories abound.

Some maintain that he fell off his horse during a pursuit

from Egypt, due to severe injuries.

Others claim that he was felled by a protracted bout of pneumonia.

The Galician–Volhyman Chronicle deemed he was killed by the Tanguts in battle, after he had taken a Tangut princess as war booty.

Many local myths suggest the princess herself had hidden a small dagger, and at the appropriate moment in his love-making, stabbed him.

There are no theories that he had died of a nosebleed.

He left firm instructions that were to be followed after his death; an unmarked grave according to the customs of his original tribe.

The funeral escort killed anyone in their path who could possibly have witnessed his burial, and the site remains unknown.

SHE EATS

HER LOVER AFTER MATING, THEN LIKES TO SWALLOW A SNAKE.

IF YOU ARE ANYTHING LIKE ME, YOU WOULD vomit in terror and promptly pass out at the sight of the spider shown here.

Equally, I would weep with panic if ever confronted by the gruesome snake that has become its victim.

This stomach-churning spectacle greeted receptionist Tania Robertson in South Africa one morning as she returned to her desk.

She calmly reached for her camera and took a series of photographs showing the snake being simultaneously eaten and rolled up into a manageable bite-size ball by the Brown Button spider.

The Brown Button is a cousin of the Black Widow; their bites are certainly exceptionally painful for humans, but contrary to popular belief, will not kill immediately.

DEAD   15

Black Widow spiders gained their brand name due to their sexual cannibalism; eating their mate post coitus, biting into their lover and starting to tuck in as they begin to achieve conclusion.

Is this perhaps the most eloquent of nature's illustration of female appetites?

As a nightmarish way of dying, being eaten alive, stung to death, or ripped to shreds by wild animals is probably high on most people's lists – especially if horror movies are a fair indication of our deepest fears.

From giant anacondas, hungry sharks, killer insects, resurrected dinosaurs and even birds, the animal kingdom has provided Hollywood with ample baddies.

Perhaps the success of these movies lies in their appeal to our primordial sense of anxiety about the dangers of the natural world, handed down to us from our ancient cave-dwelling ancestors.

Gathered around a campfire at night, with little to protect you save a crude spear or a wooden club, the howls of animals nearby would have inspired chilling dread, and probably convinced us that tribal living was the best strategy for survival.

Today the animal kingdom is held at arm's length, and our most common interactions are with domestic pets.

However the unnerving trepidation lives on, mediated and magnified through film and adventure books.

The effect of *Jaws* on the popular conception of sharks is well documented, and this creature, perfectly honed through millennia of evolution, has come to occupy a totemic position in our nightmares.

Sharks, of course, come rather low on compilations of the world's leading assassins.

Less than one person a year dies via a shark attack in the U.S. whilst the furry friends we actively invite into our homes are

responsible for 31 deaths a year.

Pitbull dogs are notoriously unstable companions, followed by Rottweilers and Huskies.

The deadliest killers by far in the U.S. are bees and wasps. Those who are allergic run the risk of death by anaphylactic shock, whilst the rest of us still face the danger of complications caused by multiple stings.

The continent of North America is rather tame compared to the creatures that roam the savannahs of Africa, or scuttle across the scorched earth of Australia.

Bill Bryson's Outback guide *In A Sunburned Country*, provides a perfect insight into the vicious neighbours living alongside you. "It has more things that will kill you than anywhere else on Earth. Of the world's ten most poisonous snakes, all are Australian. Five of its creatures – the funnel web spider, box jellyfish, blueringed octopus, paralysis tick, and stonefish – are

DEAD   17

the most lethal of their type in the world. It's a tough place".

But it is the global scourge of mankind's most fearsome enemy – the remorseless mosquito – that accounts for most fatalities.

This whining parasite carries infections from host to host, mixing blood of the well and unwell, and spreading diseases such as West Nile virus, tularemia, dengue fever, yellow fever and malaria across continents.

Malaria alone is inflicted on 247 million people worldwide each year, and routinely costs one million lives.

The oceans have been a remarkably rich environment for the development of natural born killers.

Jellyfish kill over 100 people each year, and the king of these is the Box variety, the most venomous creature in the world.

Their toxic stringy tentacles hang up to ten feet in length, handy for wrapping around limbs of swimmers.

The sting is so painful that there have been reports of victims blacking-out from the agony, but continuing to scream whilst unconscious.

Shock alone usually causes heart failure, and if you are fortunate enough to survive a glancing contact, the pain is continuous for weeks.

Scientists believe that the reason the Box jellyfish have developed such powerful venom, when they have no need to kill anything larger than the shrimps they feed on, is their need to stun their prey instantaneously in order to avoid any thrashing around damaging their delicate tendrils.

What are Box jellyfish afraid of?

Sea turtles are the only predator of these little monsters, because their thick skin provides protection from the venom.

Whole species aside, there are certain individual animals who have picked up a taste for human flesh, and become terrifying foes; one of these can be found in the war-torn country Burundi.

Named Gustave, this large male Nile crocodile is rumoured to have killed and devoured 300 humans around the shores of Lake Tanganyika.

He is a magnificent 6 metres in length, and is scarred by three bullet holes – testament to his superpowers.

Patrice Faye, a herpetologist, has been studying Gustave since the 90s and hopes to capture him in order to keep him safe from vengeful locals and poachers.

Some speculate that his enormous size is what drives him to hunt humans – and even hippos; he is simply not nimble enough to hunt the small fish that crocodiles usually feed on.

He sounds athletic enough to me, but if Mr Faye desires to, he is welcome to keep him as a pet – but not in my suburb of London please.

THERE WERE FEWER GUNFIGHTS IN THE WILD WEST THAN IN DETROIT TODAY.

HOLLYWOOD BELIEVES THE WILD WEST WAS full of gunslingers, buffalo hunters, the U.S. Cavalry, bank robbers, gold prospectors and lonesome cowboys – all-American, all-white folk heroes.

In reality the Old West was more like a multicultural melting pot, comparable to 21st Century New York or London.

Rock Springs in Wyoming was recorded as having 56 nationalities, in a population of less than 10,000 people.

And the brutality of the shoot-outs were exaggerated and romanticised, with relish.

Henry McCarty was born in 1859 and died at the age of twenty-one.

Commonly remembered as Billy the Kid, he was one of the most vicious outlaws and killers of the Wild West.

Yet his reputation of a man with 'inborn savagery' appears somewhat inflated, given that he only ever shot four people.

The magic of cinema and television ensures that the legend of the Wild West continues to be mythologised by the dominant and enduring icons; Clint Eastwood in his poncho, Elvis Presley in cowboy leathers and holster, even Roy Rogers and his horse Trigger, "riding tonight, returning to our silver screens" as the Elton John song recounts.

The Wild West is notorious for its swinging saloon doors and quick-draw gunfighters twirling their pistols before a casual afternoon shoot-out.

In truth the highest number of gunshot murders the entire Wild West saw in a year was five.

Most towns averaged 1.5 murders a year, and not of all of these were caused by firearms.

You are more likely to be murdered in Detroit today, which recently suffered its highest recorded homicide count in two decades; 55 homicides per 100,000 residents that year.

It is accepted that the United States has the largest rate of gun ownership in the world, with 89 guns for every 100 Americans, compared to 6 in England and Wales.

Ironically, the UK's number is inflated by the number of armed guards who man the American Embassy in London.

In Britain official figures record on average around 550 murders per year.

At the last tally, there were 12,664 recorded murders annually in the U.S., of which 8,583 were caused by firearms.

The Wild West was a period of rapid and dramatic expansion, littered with unfulfilled treaties and the vast slaughter of countless indigenous tribes, "massacres disguised as battles" against the Native American Indians.

At the time the many atrocities committed were concealed, but new research suggests the term 'American Indian holocaust' is an apt description.

It challenges the historical amnesia concerning the wiping out of 90% of an estimated 50 to 100 million Native Indians who originally inhabited the North American plains.

In 1863, even during the U.S. Civil War, at the Bear River massacre four hundred and fifty members of the Shoshone tribe were shot to death by federal troops from California.

Gunshot homicide continues to constitute a significant part of the infrastructure of contemporary American society; 70% of murders recorded in California during recent years were by firearm.

However, nowhere in America comes close to San Pedro Sula in Honduras, considered to have one of the world's grimmest murder rates.

According to the U.N., San Pedro notches up over three killings a day in its comparatively tiny area; it sounds a fearsome place indeed.

But Americans are trying hard to keep up.

William Rainey Harper High School is located on the Southside of Chicago, Illinois; in 2012 during the space of a year, 27 students were delivered severe or fatal injuries from gunshots.

Everyone's favourite gunslinger from the Old West was Annie Oakley, 5 feet tall, an entertainer, and a legendary markswoman.

If a playing card was tossed into the air 90 feet away, Annie could hit the card with five or six shots before it settled on the ground.

This was no magic trick; one day, using a rifle, she hit 4,472 out of 5,000 glass marbles tossed into the air.

Perhaps she was the inspiration for today's Bolivian women, increasing numbers of whom want to show that they can dominate in a male speciality. They too have become entertainers, wrestling in the top flight in the rings traditionally dominated by burly males.

Carmen Rosa is a local Aymara woman. In the daytime she works in a restaurant but when she finishes work she heads to the outskirts of La Paz.

Here, she and other female wrestlers wearing colourful dresses, layers of petticoats and pretty hats, fight against dominant

machismo and discrimination, bringing Bolivia's most feared male wrestlers to the ground with their bare hands, using individually crafted techniques, and wily cunning.

I miss the grandeur of the classic John Ford westerns, although every few years Hollywood still produces a cracking one – not a *High Noon* perhaps, but *Unforgiven*, *True Grit*, *Django Unchained* are far more thrilling than almost all current shoot-em-up action 'thrillers'.

My favourite of the Wild West legends was Cherokee Bill's sardonic comment on the gallows, in response to the hangman who asked if he had any last words.

"Hell no, I came here to die, not to make a speech".

†

Note: Tombstone still attracts tourists who want to see the deadliest town in the Old West. However, its record number of gun deaths in a single year was three; in most years during the Wild West era, not a single gunfight fatality was recorded. It is obviously good business to perpetuate the myths of quick-draw gunslingers duelling in the streets, and deadly shoot-outs in every saloon from Dodge City to Deadwood.

Books, comics, and Hollywood westerns have built on the legend, attracting an endless supply of visitors to the iconic towns of the cowboy era.

Of course, today's homicide capitals in America have no desire to inflate the tally of hundreds of people routinely killed by gunfire.

The gun-death charts are currently led by Chicago, New Orleans, Kansas City and Philadelphia.

THE MOST SUICIDAL PEOPLE IN THE WORLD? DOCTORS IN GREENLAND.

GREENLAND POSSESSES THE HIGHEST recorded suicide rate in the world, with 1 out of 5 citizens attempting to kill themselves at some point in their lives.

But suicide is generally far from uncommon everywhere, particularly amongst medical practitioners.

Doctors, dentists, psychiatrists are prominent on the lists of suicidal professions.

More people worldwide, one million each year, die from their own hand rather than from war.

Cruelly, more American soldiers die from committing suicide post-war, than on the front line.

Not surprisingly, the majority of suicides are related to a variety of mental imbalances, or are the consequence of drug abuse.

The world's landmark bridges have always been popular destinations to end your life, tumbling dozens of feet to a certain death.

But sometimes fallers survive, albeit suffering from internal bleeding, fractured lungs and broken spines.

In 1885, after a lovers' quarrel, Sarah Ann Henley, a young barmaid, bid farewell to her sorrow and leapt off Clifton Suspension Bridge, in Bristol.

As she dropped the 250ft, the air inside her crinoline skirt parachuted her down safely onto the water's muddy bank.

She later married in 1890 and lived to be 85 years old, ever grateful to the fashionable outfit she chose for her suicide attempt.

French actress Simone Mareuil was best known for her appearance in the surrealist film *Un Chien Andalou*.

But she became globally renowned in 1954, when her clinical depression overcame her reason; she covered her body in gasoline and then set fire to herself, surrounded by horrified passers-by in a public square.

Jim Jones was the founder and leader of the notorious cult, The People's Temple at Jonestown, Guyana.

On 18 November 1978, 909 suicides were committed within the community, almost all of them by cyanide poisoning.

During this mass insanity over 200 children died at Jonestown.

This resulted in the largest number of American civilian deaths, other than those caused by natural disaster, until 11 September 2001.

Jim Jones described these deaths as 'Revolutionary Suicides'.

He also believed that he was the reincarnation of the 'anarchists' Gandhi, Jesus, Buddha, and Lenin.

He was found with a self-inflicted fatal gunshot to the head.

In Japan, *The Complete Manual of Suicide* written by Wataru Tsurumi was first published in 1993, and sold more than a million copies.

It provides graphic descriptions of how to complete your suicide correctly and effectively. The Japanese government did not censor the book's content in any way.

It features eleven methods of suicide: overdosing, hanging, self-defenestration, cutting wrists, car collision, gas poisoning, electrocution, drowning, self-immolation, freezing – and a chapter on miscellaneous other options you might be interested in pursuing.

This D.I.Y. suicide book rates the scale of pain and the guaranteed lethality of each technique, using images of skulls, with five skulls illustrate the highest rating.

The manual has been found beside the bodies of many suicide victims.

In 1933 two girls in their early twenties, Mieko Ueki and Masako Tomita climbed to the top of the volcano Mihara-Yama, on the island of Oshima, in Japan.

Mieko told Masako how she was enchanted by the legend that the bodies of those who jumped into the burning lava would be instantly cremated, and sent up to the heavens in the form of smoke.

Mieko intended to commit suicide as the fable had described and after the two girls bowed to each other, Mieko then leaped into the crater.

Japan was in the midst of an economic depression and as quickly as her story became folklore, Mihara-Yama became a suicide destination and a national tourist attraction.

That year 143 people copied Mieko's suicide.

Two new steamboats were bought to ferry tourists to the volcano.

A post office was built at the crater's edge, so tourists could be simultaneously disturbed and fascinated as they watched someone commit suicide, and then pick up a souvenir postcard.

Jack Kevorkian, named by critics as 'Dr Death', was a pathologist who became widely known in America for his activism backing voluntary euthanasia.

He built a suicide machine, which operated from inside a Volkswagen van. It challenged social taboos and national views towards assisted-suicide. A lethal drug dose would be automatically injected into the arm, but controlled by the patient choosing to press a button.

Beginning in 1990, he claimed to have assisted 130 suicides.

He served eight years in prison, but after being released was able to enjoy watching Al Pacino portraying him in the film *You Don't Know Jack*, which won several awards.

The much admired writer who fearsomely resisted growing old was Hunter S. Thompson, author of *Fear and Loathing in Las Vegas*.

He killed himself by gunshot in 2005.

His suicide note read "No More Games. No More Bombs. No More Walking. No More Fun. No More Swimming. 67. That is 17 years past 50. 17 More than I needed or wanted. Boring. I am always bitchy. No Fun… Act your old age…"

†

Note: The Aokigahara forest at the base of Mount Fuji in Japan is the most popular suicide location in the world.

In the density of the countless trees, corpses hang from

branches on homemade nooses; surrounding them are many official signs displaying messages such as "Life is a precious thing!" "Please reconsider!" and "Think of your family!"

You may also run into scavengers searching the bodies for any cash, watches or jewellery.

It became a fashionable destination for severely depressed teenagers in the 1950s, and it has achieved mythic status amongst the suicidal ever since.

Some accounts maintain the forest was already known as the Hanging Trees centuries ago, and interest was rekindled in the aftermath of post war trauma.

A GOOD DEATH.

IT CANNOT BE EASY FOR HOLLYWOOD, after decades of providing us with many final scenes in which a leading protagonist is killed off – acres of celluloid shootings, knifings, poisonings, of having victims being polished off by monsters, savage beasts, homicidal maniacs, rabid vampires – to find ways to accomplish a fresh kill.

A memorable death must now be original enough and graphic enough to retain the power to grip you, despite horror movies making even the goriest and grisliest of murders as simply mundane.

A good death demands perfectionism whether it be operatic in scale, or eerily minimalist; violent brutality and mayhem is the province of the hack, unless he happens to be Sam Peckinpah filming *The Wild Bunch*.

Alfred Hitchcock killed poor Janet Leigh in her shower with such skillful cinematography, cutting from the bath plughole to her cold lifeless eye, it rendered all the slasher movies that it influenced utterly redundant.

Brian de Palma used *Scarface* to prove he could still find a way to kill its hero Montana in an endless hail of bullets, riddling his body as memorably as Bonnie and Clyde's, or Sonny

in *The Godfather*, in the earlier films. De Palma also gave Donald Sutherland a truly shocking demise in *Don't Look Now*.

Tarantino is a master of spectacularly unexpected deaths; Uma Thurman finally finishes of Bill after five hours of *Kill Bill* Part 1 and 2, using no weapon other than her hand, employing the Five Point Palm Exploding Heart Technique.

Stanley Kubrick was an unsurpassed craftsman of death scenes, in particular his troubled Private Pyle dying in the barracks' bathroom in *Full Metal Jacket*, or the axe buried in Scatman Crother's chest by Jack Nicholson in *The Shining*, or Major TJ plummeting to his doom riding on an atom bomb, waving his cowboy hat in the finale of *Dr Strangelove*.

Spielberg gave us two corkers: The massive T-Rex gulping down Gennaro as he sits on his lavatory bowl, and Robert

DEAD   31

Shaw succumbing to his nemesis, the giant shark in *Jaws*.

You wouldn't want to watch Ridley Scott's *Hannibal* while enjoying a TV dinner; agent Clarice Starling has to look on as Lecter removes the top of Ray Liotta's skull, cuts out a section of his brain and then feeds it to his still talkative guest.

A fine death indeed.

Ridley Scott also offered us the electrifying sight of the alien squirming its way out from inside John Hurt's stomach; Scott was inconsiderate enough not to tell the cast members in the scene gathered around Hurt what was about to happen – that way, he could capture their shock and revulsion in all its authenticity.

In Scott's *Blade Runner*, his Ray the Replicant is the process of killing Harrison Ford when he surprisingly saves him from falling from a rooftop.

Ray tells us of his anguish at being a mere replicant and not truly human, quietly dying when his life force extinguishes, as though his non-Duracell batteries have run out.

Heath Ledger transfixed an otherwise routine Batman film, *The Dark Knight* when his Joker ambles in to a meeting of mobsters, asking "How about a magic trick?" He then makes a pencil disappear – by slamming it inside someone's forehead, announcing "Ta dah!"

Probably the most haunting of all movie deaths was never actually shown on screen – the shooting of Bambi's mother. No scene in Hollywood history has brought more tears to more eyes.

I can't remember having a good cry at any literary death.

Oscar Wilde was right as always in reporting that you would need a heart of stone not to laugh at the passing of Little Nell, or the Tullivers in *The Mill on the Floss*, as they clamber on each other to save themselves as they drown in the powerful river.

Of course, they were vile, unlike Nell, who took so many chapters to be extinguished in Dickens' *The Old Curiosity Shop*, most readers will have been relieved by her final dispatch.

But his Sydney Carton was probably one of the most resonant of cultivated demises in *A Tale of Two Cities*.

Even an exceptionally manly reader would have been moved by the death of dear Heathcliff in *Wuthering Heights* – he was so grandly stoic despite his burdensome inner turmoils.

Everyone has their own favourite bookish deaths – even if they made grim reading at the time.

Thomas Hardy's Henchard in *The Mayor of Casterbridge*, Svidrigailov in *Crime and Punishment*, Julius Caesar, Jo in *Bleak House*, Beth in *Little Women*, the rabbit whose name I have forgotten in *Watership Down*, the magnificent Madame Bovary.

Didn't just about everybody die in *A Hundred Years of Solitude*?

But let us not forget the unrivalled death in the best-selling book of all time – Jesus.

My favourite passing? Why, Ronald Nimkin of course, and his endearingly thoughtful suicide in Philip Roth's great *Portnoy's Complaint*.

You never forget his farewell note to his mother "Mrs Blumenthal called. Please bring your mah-jong rules to the game tonight."

WHEN·HUMANS·BECOME·EXTINCT, WHO·WILL·RULE·THE EARTH?

WHAT DOES DOOMSDAY LOOK LIKE? EVER since humanity emerged from the slime and founded systems of belief, various apocalypse scenarios have been used to bring populations to heel and kept in fear of the gods.

From hellfire and torture, to demons walking the earth, the end of days have never sounded very appealing. The newest theories of the extinction of the human race arc no more so.

Most religions visualise the end of the world as being brought about by divine intervention – good news for the devout, bad news for sinners.

Contemporary predictions place humanity firmly at the centre of its own demise.

Albert Einstein issued the gloomy conclusion, "Man has lost the capacity to foresee and to forestall. He will end up destroying the Earth".

Climate change enthusiasts cling to this statement as referring to our ever-increasing output of carbon dioxide, tipping us over the tipping-point scientists have pinpointed as central to complete environmental disaster.

Believers in the ensuing planetary chaos predict an Anoxic event, something that took place in the Jurassic and Paleozoic times, when the oceans become devoid of oxygen, leading to the widespread death of marine animals – a food source for billions.

DEAD   35

Areas of ocean have appeared around the world in which there is not enough oxygen to support life.

The first stirrings of these show telltale signs such as algal blooms and clouds of jellyfish.

Aside from the impact mankind's activities may have on the environment, there is of course the possibility of Omnicide, or human extinction due to human action such as widespread nuclear or biological warfare.

Our propensity to violence as a species would seem to point to this – Jared Diamond, an influential anthropologist, has recorded our similarity to other primates in this tendency, and estimates that 64% of hunter-gatherer societies make war every few years.

Other thinkers suggest that the future is not so grim.

Harvard psychologist Steven Pinker has offered statistical

DEAD

analysis of violence globally and found that the number of people killed in battle has dropped 1,000-fold over the centuries, and that fewer people are murdered.

He cites the main reasons for this drop as being that our IQs are developing and we attach more value to human life as a result.

Others insist that we are devolving as a species – indeed both HG Wells' *Time Machine* and Aldous Huxley's *Brave New World* predicted futures in which humanity has fallen into a state of idiocy and backwardness.

Overpopulation stands as one of the most worrying extinction theories.

With the world's population now over 7 billion, (it has doubled in the past 50 years) the competition for resources will intensify.

The conclusions drawn are of increased instability, disease and the exhaustion of the soil and sea.

Leading climate-change pessimists like Professor Frank Fenner, an award-winning emeritus professor of microbiology, believes it's already too late.

He claims that we'll be extinct within the next 100 years due to man's reckless disregard for the planet, and the demands of an ever-growing population.

The joy of having so many experts, abounding with compelling viewpoints, conversely provides us with many equally respected analysts who fret about depopulation.

Throughout the 'advanced' world there has emerged a preference for fewer children; indeed if population levels fall to the current rate that Germany is experiencing, we would be facing a soft extinction by 2400.

Some conspiracy theorists firmly propose that there is currently a concerted effort amongst the shady elite powers that run the globe to reduce world populations.

Their chief tools are war, weather modification, the spread of disease and withholding of cures.

Our own Prince Phillip seems to be in on the scheme, having publicly stated "If I were reincarnated, I would wish to be returned to Earth as a killer virus to lower human population levels".

Technically named 'sub-replacement generative capacity' populations are declining in countries such as China, Japan, Italy.

Whilst depopulation may have some positive effects, it touches on a lurking threat to humanity in the form of dropping fertility rates, as fictionalised in the book, and later film, *Children of Men*.

Research in this area remains controversial, but paranoia seekers suggest serious falls in male potency, affected by chemicals in the water supply.

Before we all panic bear in mind dinosaurs managed to inhabit the earth for 135 million years; if we are to match them we have a long way to go yet.

The first members of the human family made their entry between 6 and 7 million years ago, homo sapiens proper have been around for a paltry 1.9–2.4 million years, and modern humans evolved in East Africa around 200,000 years ago, merely the blink of an eye.

The universe has bigger time spans in mind, and those will be unequivocal in their annihilation of our little rock.

Solar flares, rogue black holes, gamma ray bursts (or more excitingly, an alien invasion) could all reach out from the darkness to destroy life on Earth.

In a million years Eta Carinae will go hypernova.

In 1.4 million years the Oort cloud will be disturbed, sending a hail of comets our way.

In 1 billion years the oceans will evaporate under the brightening of the sun, as it grows into a bigger Red Giant.

In 3 billion years we will collide with the Andromeda galaxy.

But no doubt, as we all know, cockroaches are indestructible, and will finally take their place as rulers of whatever is left.

PERFECT HEALTH IS MERELY THE SLOWEST WAY TO DIE.

THE THOUGHT OF BECOMING A CENTENARIAN is not necessarily a pleasant one.

With prospects of physical and mental decline, you will also live to bear witness to many of your family and friends dying around you.

But former postman Jiroemon Kimura, born in Japan on 19 April 1897, celebrated his 116th and final birthday sitting up watching TV in bed and appeared delighted to be named the world's oldest person by the Guinness World Records. However, China challenged this claim and felt that the honour belonged to Luo Meizhen, photographed here, who was 127 years old when she died in June 2013. Despite Ms Meizhen possessing an ID card, which certified that she was born in 1885, she did not have a birth certificate, and so could not officially be crowned the world's oldest person.

With 12,000 centenarians in the UK alone and an estimated 316,600 living worldwide, people seeking very long lives are desperate to discover the clues to their hardiness. In *Secrets To Living A Long Life From Centenarians*, Samuel Ball, at 102 years old revealed that he believes to live long, you need to

40   DEAD

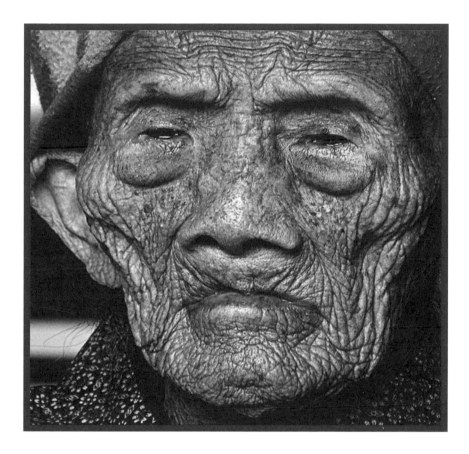

enjoy life's pleasures, "have a good wife, two scotches a night, and be easy going".

In 1921, psychologist Lewis Terman began *The Longevity Project*, which would outlive him and last eight decades. He selected promising young children as his subjects and followed them into adulthood, discovering that a high IQ doesn't play a significant role in living a lengthy life. Rather he found that persistence, stubbornness, and the ability to navigate life's challenges are a better indication of those destined for an extended lifespan, revealed even from an early age.

The study also learned that women who are sexually satisfied and climax more frequently often have higher life expectancy than those who don't. It is certainly the case that 85% of centenarians are female.

A straightforward view came from Besse Cooper, who at 116 told people to simply "mind your own business and don't eat junk food". Jean Calmect, who died in 1997 at age 122 never let her age get in the way of doing whatever she wanted. She took up fencing at 85, rode her bicycle till she was 100, and didn't give up smoking till she was 117.

Vivian Henscheke, 109, also smoked for most of her life, and "never exercised a single day, and ate whatever she wanted" according to her daughter, 86. Cheerful Bel Kaufman, revealed at 101 that "laughter keeps you healthy. You can survive by seeing humour in everything. Thumb your nose at sadness; turn the tables on tragedy."

Bel's advice was taken to heart by Oxford University, whose research study decreed that laughing really is good for your health. Happy outbursts of laughter encourage the human body to release endorphins which stimulate an exaggerated physical state of euphoria.

But be warned: laughter can also kill you. Instances of laughing to death have been recorded from Ancient Greece to the 21st Century, with victims suffering muscle failure, seizures and cardiac arrest.

In 1975 Alex Mitchell died whilst watching the 'Kung Fu Kapers' episode of *The Goodies*. Laughing uncontrollably for twenty-five minutes, he died from a heart attack. Following his death, his wife Nessie sent the trio of comedians Tim Brooke-Taylor, Graeme Garden and Bill Oddie a letter to thank them for making his dying moments so happy.

More recently, in 2003 ice-cream salesman Damnoen Saenum died whilst laughing in his sleep. His wife tried to wake him, but after two minutes of continuous laughter he stopped breathing. He had died from asphyxiation and heart collapse.

Ikaria is the Greek island named after the story of Icarus, son of Daedalus. Father and son were imprisoned in Crete and to escape, Daedalus designed two pairs of wings from feathers and beeswax.

Ignoring his father's warning not to fly too close to the sun, Icarus' wings melted and with his feathers unbinding, he plunged to his death in the Ikarian sea.

Despite Ancient Greece being renowned for its mythological tales of tragedy and death, it is no myth that the inhabitants of Ikaria live on average for ten years longer than the rest of Western Europe.

But perhaps Dionysus, God of Wine, still preserves the lives of Ikaria's 8,000 inhabitants. Stamatis Mortaitis, aged 98, still tends 200 olive trees and produces about 700 litres of red wine a year.

45 years ago he was diagnosed in the U.S. with terminal lung cancer, and given nine months to live. He wanted to die on the island on which he was born, and returned.

He is still very much alive, and believes it's because there are no preservatives in his wine, and that Ikaria's grapes are blessed with life enhancing properties. A few years ago he went to the U.S. in search of his doctors; he couldn't find them, as they were all dead.

The islanders' longevity may be consequence of many factors. Their Mediterranean diet consists of fish, vegetables and very little red meat, and it is mainly cooked in what many consider to be the world's finest olive oil.

Others credit the island's speciality, a boiled Greek local coffee which is rich in antioxidants, and low in caffeine; apparently it strengthens the cells that surround blood vessels, lowering cardiovascular problems.

Ikaria's mountainous terrain has meant that most people aged over ninety remain physically active. Extended families result in older inhabitants having important roles in the community. With active social lives, levels of depression and dementia are comparatively low compared to other parts of Western Europe.

Religious food taboos have traditionally regarded certain species as unclean to eat and unhealthy for the soul. Hindus do not eat beef and Jews, Moslems, and Seventh Day Adventists don't eat pork.

But could the secret to a long life be bacon? Pearl Cantrell, from Richard Springs, Texas believes that eating bacon every day is the reason she has lived to be 105. A full English breakfast of bacon and eggs, despite dietary criticism, is somewhat surprisingly considered by many physicians to be the ideal start to each morning, increasing your metabolism and allowing your body to break down food more effectively during the rest of the day.

This doesn't stop many observers suspecting that high cholesterol and blood pressure to be a greater cause of death during the 20th century than decades of global wars.

Rather quaintly, a chart of mortality data over the last hundred years reveals that 19 million fewer lives have been lost in civil wars around the world than deaths caused by people falling over accidentally.

RVN OVER BY YOVR OWN CAR, BEING DRIVEN BY YOVR OWN DOG.

JAMES CAMPBELL WAS RETURNING HOME after running some errands with his wife.

He was backing his car into their driveway, and as he stepped out to open the garage door their pet bulldog jumped inside the car and decided to press the accelerator. Before his wife could do anything about it, the vehicle had already run over her husband, killing him instantly.

What pet did you have as a child? A faithful hound? Disinterested guinea pig? Or perhaps a Black Widow Spider?

Owners of bizarre pets seem to abound in the U.S., and many of them meet gruesome ends. The belief that we have some kind of mystical connection to the animal kingdom, and that wild creatures can become our best friends is patently untrue.

Animals which rely on us for sustenance will tolerate us in a strategic manner, should they have docile natures. Taking a wild animal, whose every genetic fibre strains to attack, maim and kill, and put it into a domestic environment is simply asking for trouble.

If you live in the UK you are most likely to have a rather pedestrian pet – the humble fish. Small, relatively low maintenance and decorative, they remain deeply popular – there are over 6 million in the UK.

For some, this is not nearly enough excitement.

DEAD   45

Estimates suggest that in the U.S. there are more tigers in captivity than in the entirety of Asia.

In 2011, Terry Thompson was found dead at his property in Ohio. He had shot himself, after releasing all of the animals on his farm from their enclosures.

This menagerie included lions, tigers and bears. Local police turned into poachers as the terrified townspeople were advised to stay home.

They shot and killed eighteen Bengal tigers, seventeen lions, six black bears, two grizzlies, three mountain lions and a baboon.

Thompson had earlier been fined for ill-treatment of his animals, so was known to authorities.

Despite this he was still allowed to keep a small zoo on his property.

His death, and the ensuing safari hunt, was a turning point for exotic pet ownership in the U.S.; it brought into the spotlight the booming industry in domestic breeding of wild animals – a tiger cub can command $700, a giraffe $25,000 – and apparently tigers are remarkably easy to breed.

A visit to exoticanimalsforsale.net will show just how widespread the trade is.

Eight states in the U.S. have no laws at all applicable to owning unusual animals; other states appear quite accommodating – in Colorado you can own up to six kangaroos.

This laxity in Federal Law, and the consequent high rate of wild pet ownership has resulted in 75 deaths since 1990, and over 1,500 serious injuries.

A number of unconventional pets have to be taken into wildlife sanctuaries when their owners run out of money to keep them, or simply lose interest.

Financial difficulties are at the core of a tragic story that took place in Florida – the state with the highest pet-induced fatalities.

Couple Jaren Hare and Charles Darnell kept a giant albino python in their home. The reptile was kept in a glass box, secured on top by nothing more than a duvet and some bungee chords.

The snake was apt to escape and roam the house. It had not been fed for over a month as its owners had no money to buy it food; its last meal had been a squirrel the Darnells had found killed on a nearby highway.

One morning the couple awoke to find the python wrapped around their two year old daughter, its fangs embedded fatally into her forehead.

Darnell stabbed the python multiple times, but it was clearly too late to save the child.

The couple went on trial for manslaughter, their negligence deemed criminal. The snake survived, and now lives in a wild-life centre.

In 2011 newspapers reported the death of Marius Els, a 40-year-old army major who was bitten to death by his 1.2 tonne pet hippopotamus.

Els had attempted to domesticate the beast on his farm in the Free State province, totally disregarding his wife's and friends' entreaties that this beast could never be tamed.

Els persevered, and indeed was known to ride on his hippo's back.

Named Humphrey, the hippopotamus had been saved as a baby from flood waters, and was adopted by Els for whom the creature rapidly became 'like a son'. Humphrey became more aggressive as he grew, terrorising two canoeists who had to take to a tree for escape, and attacking calves on the farm. Els was eventually found bitten to death and floating in the lake he had built for the hippo.

A particularly grisly story concerned a young man living in Dortmund with a penchant for lizards and snakes.

Mark Voegel, 30, was found dead in his apartment, after neighbours had alerted the police when the smell from his home became overpowering.

On entering the police were faced with a nightmarish sight. Voegel had been bitten by his pet Black Widow spider, named Bettina, and died sprawled over the sofa. Snakes, spiders, lizards and termites had feasted on his body, spinning webs and tearing flesh away from his bones.

On analysing the home, officials found that the heated tanks housing his pets had developed an electrical fuse, burning away portions of the cages to let their inhabitants free. One wildlife expert commented that Voegel had been living among spiders with the highest aggression rates in the species.

Note: Dogs can make excellent drivers.

In New Zealand the organisation that protects animals from cruelty wanted to demonstrate that the dogs they rescue may have been abandoned, abused, and forgotten – but can still be highly intelligent.

Aiming to clear up misconceptions about the dogs, and help them find new homes, they explained "sometimes people think that because they are getting an animal that was neglected and dumped, somehow it is second-class".

Driving a car demonstrates to potential adopters that a dog that has fallen on hard times still has potential as a family pet, bright and alert enough to enjoy playing and learning new tricks.

The animals are trained in real cars, modified to accommodate their needs, receiving verbal commands as guidance.

Now, they drive their Mini Countrymans confidently, and unassisted.

HAUNTED FOREVER BY YOUR OWN LAST WORDS.

NOBODY LIKES THE IDEA OF THEIR LAST words being something vile said to a loved one, in the middle of a heated exchange.

Nevertheless if you have a penchant for memorable final utterances, you will probably know two of my favourites:

†

Well, gentlemen, you are about to see a baked Appel.
GEORGE APPEL, EXECUTED BY ELECTRIC CHAIR, 1928.

†

How about this for a headline for tomorrow's paper? French Fries!
JAMES FRENCH, EXECUTED BY ELECTRIC CHAIR, 1966.

A man or woman's last words can be read as the perfect encapsulation of their approach to life.

Gallows humour is particularly resonant, as the two quotes above can attest. For a person situated on threshold of death, their life about to be taken from them by others, and yet able to make a light-hearted observation, is a remarkable testament to the human condition.

Sigmund Freud made a study of this particular form of humour, and formulated the following theory; "The ego refuses

DEAD

to be distressed by the provocations of reality, to let itself be compelled to suffer".

Gallows humour appears to be the absolute refusal to bow to the wretchedness of your suffering, a final grasping of power by the powerless.

Kurt Vonnegut, the great novelist, pinpoints the evolution of Gallows humour to a time far before Freud turned to it.

He sees it as a Middle European humour, developed as a response to desperation.

"It's humour from the Peasants' Revolt, the Thirty Years' War, and from the Napoleonic battles. It's small people being pushed this way and that…and still hanging on in the face of hopelessness."

Gallows humour he sees as a revolutionary force, the mark of an individual or group who will not yield to the stronger powers that threaten them.

Shakespearean England was no stranger to this form of wry acceptance of your fate, and given the number of executions that took place during the time, perhaps that is little surprise.

When Sir Walter Raleigh was offered to examine the axe to test it for sharpness before his beheading, he commented "This is a sharp Medicine, but it is a Physician for all diseases and miseries".

Shakespeare himself would have been proud of such a phrase, and it certainly evokes a spirit that enters into many of his plays.

In *Romeo and Juliet* the stabbed Mercutio utters his final line "No, 'tis not so deep as a well, nor so wide as a church-door; but 'tis enough, 'twill serve: ask for me to-morrow, and you shall find me a grave man".

Black comedy – a form of gallows humour in which the object of laughter is a third party rather than yourself – also runs through English literature and arts.

The French surrealist, André Breton, coined the term 'humour noir' and credited Jonathan Swift as the main proponent of the form.

Swift's barbed and savage brand of wit is nowhere better exemplified than in *A Modest Proposal* and *A Meditation on a Broomstick*.

In the latter he satirised a popular religious text, meditating on household objects as metaphors for our relationship with God.

Gallows comedy continues to run throughout contemporary culture, nowhere better expressed than in *Monty Python's Life of Brian*.

In the film, victims of crucifixion begin to sing *Always Look on the Bright Side of Life*.

This sentiment is so dear to Britain that the song was sung at the closing of the 2012 Olympics.

The form is truly international however. In France it is also called *rire jaune*, which literally translates as 'yellow humour'.

There, it has a slightly different and less revolutionary meaning, with a sense of forcing yourself to laugh, the yellow colour standing for a liverish bile.

As such this form of forced laughter is used to try and calm oneself down when trying not to show anger. In Belgium it is called *groen lachen*, which literally translates as 'to laugh desperately'.

Gallows humour has been also connected strongly with the Jewish communities of Eastern Europe, a point emphasised by Vonnegut, was imported into the U.S. and Russia with the movement of Jews across those continents.

A disproportionate number of popular comedy shows are written by Jewish writers, their brand of self-depreciating humour seeming to tickle funny bones internationally.

Gallows humour within the Jewish community about anti-Semitism seems to perform a task of coping with prejudice before it is actively applied.

For example, the following ironic joke: "During the days of oppression and poverty of the Russian shtetls, one village had a rumour going around: a Christian girl was found murdered near their village.

Fearing a pogrom, they gathered at the synagogue. Suddenly, the rabbi came running up, and cried, 'Wonderful news! The murdered girl was Jewish!'"

The value of humour is not to be underestimated.

It has been medically demonstrated that laughter boosts the flow of blood around the body, and creates endorphins which can help relieve pain, and reduce stress hormones.

Indeed laughter can even strengthen the immune system. Freud conjectured that laughter brings a healthy energy to the individual, and as such is used as a coping mechanism when one is angry, sad or upset.

DEAD 53

Nietzsche had a rather more grim prognosis, that laughter was a reaction to the sense of existential loneliness and mortality that we all daily face.

I wonder what he would have made of James French or George Appel's final comments.

DEAD

CHARLES
DARWIN KILLED EVERY
ANIMAL
HE DISCOVERED, AND ATE IT.

FROM DARWIN WE LEARN THAT ARMADILLO "tastes like duck", and that puma is "very like veal".

He found owls to be "indescribably unpleasant", but that an agouti rodent, pictured overleaf, "the best meat I ever tasted".

He couldn't resist eating the animals he was studying, and some of his discoveries were clearly too tasty to resist; of the 48 giant tortoises he brought back on the *Beagle*, not a single one survived his hearty appetite.

His delight in unusual suppers has an illustrious history.

At Cambridge University he was a member of the Glutton Club, an intrepid group of gourmands who wanted to seek out and eat "strange flesh"; their nightly raids on the animal kingdom included hawk and bittern.

However they were defeated by the encounter with stringy owl flesh, which upset all their tummies, and the group turned their attention to the more agreeable pursuit of port tasting.

Darwin and his associates were not the only Victorians with a taste for the more exotic end of the food chain.

William Buckland was one of the UK's most eminent scientists, pioneering discoveries in palaeontology; indeed he was

the first person to study geology at Oxford University.

He also was determined to eat as many species as possible, and emphatically drilled into his pupils his view that the stomach rules the world, a message often embellished with the flourish of a hyena skull.

As President of the Royal Geographical Society he was able to indulge in a number of his food obsessions by importing a wide variety of creatures into the country.

His dinner parties were legendary for their culinary extremes, with mice on toast a favourite starter.

From porpoise to panther, nothing was deemed too unappealing to sample.

Buckland displayed his desire to eat without prejudice when he visited a cathedral which had announced that a saint's blood was daily appearing on the chapel floor.

DEAD

Buckland intrepidly stooped to taste the substance, and quickly declared it bat urine.

Perhaps one of history's most remarkable eaters was a Frenchman, Tarrare, who lived in the 1700s.

This showman and soldier was turned out of his family home at a young age due to his insatiable appetite.

He particularly hungered for meat and could consume bewildering quantities of it.

Eventually be became part of a travelling troupe of performers, and would swallow increasingly bizarre items as part of his routine, including champagne corks, stones and live animals.

He joined the Revolutionary Army when war broke out, and had to scavenge amongst the dumps of Paris to supplement his meagre rations.

Accounts report that his body odour became especially unpleasant after he had eaten a gargantuan meal, and that when he was hungry his skin hung about him in folds.

Unable to harvest enough from the leftovers that were tossed into the rubbish bins outside restaurants each night, he was soon hospitalised suffering from exhaustion.

His doctors enjoyed testing his love of eating, feeding him an increasingly outlandish selection of animals.

He is recorded as eating a meal for 15 in one sitting, including live cats, snakes, lizards, and swallowed an entire live eel without chewing.

The hospital could detect no mental imbalances in Tarrare, but however much he ate he stayed at a normal weight.

On re-entering the army his talents were put to good use, as he could swallow top secret messages, and transport them securely.

Army doctors attempted to treat him yet again, this time using a concoction of tobacco pills, wine vinegar and soft-boiled eggs.

But he secretly continued to scavenge for food amongst dumps once more, even caught drinking the blood of patients in the blood-letting ward.

When a toddler disappeared at the hospital, the doctors and nurses chased Tarrare out in disgust, fearing the worst.

When he eventually died of tuberculosis, his autopsy noted that he had an abnormally wide gullet, an immense stomach riddled with ulcers, and a body full of pus.

Before the modern world distances itself from the appetites of Tarrare and Darwin, bear in mind that all kinds of meat have shown up in burgers and ready meals of late.

The horse meat scandal of 2013 rocked supermarket chains and caused giants such as Tesco and Aldi to withdraw a number of products from distribution.

Of course horse meat has been a staple across Europe and South America for years.

Nonetheless, it has been largely taboo in the UK and U.S. where we apparently have a rather more sentimental attachment to our horses.

More distressing to many are the meat samples that have been seized at British airports recently.

It was discovered that chimpanzee meat was on sale in the Midlands as part of a black market in exotic meats.

Chimp meat can fetch more than £20 per kilogram.

The first assessment into the illegal trade of wild animal meat found that over 270 tonnes of it had passed through Charles de Gaulle airport in Paris, disguised as other meat products.

Chimpanzees and apes account for less than one percent of these meats sold on the market.

What makes up the other 99% I leave to your imagination. But it gives the expression man-eating-tiger a different dimension.

CHINA,
THE·WORLD'S
BIGGEST·POPULATION,
EVEN·AFTER·100M·KILLED·EACH·OTHER.

IRONICALLY THE TAIPING REBELLION IS referred to as *Tai Ping Tian Guo* in Chinese, which translates as 'Great Kingdom of Heavenly Peace'.

It remains the bloodiest civil war ever recorded, battled between the Manchu Qing Dynasty and the Chinese 'Christian' rebels, led by Hong Xiuquan.

One of the main factors that led to the eruption of the rebellion was the large majority of the Chinese population who felt that their leadership were ineffectual; they had failed to prevent the British and French from invading during the second Opium War of 1856-60.

The Opium Wars were brutal and barbaric, and thousands of Chinese were killed in the name of free trade.

Although the Chinese had banned opium, the British were keen to acquire large quantities of tea, and began to trade it in exchange for supplying equally vast amounts of opium into China.

The social and political impact upon China was devastating, and their addiction to opium stagnated their economic and internal infrastructure.

William Jardine and James Matheson first met in a Chinese brothel. During the first Opium War in 1832 the two Scotsmen

formed the Jardine Matheson Company.

They built thirteen factories based in Canton, in southern China, one of the only areas where foreigners were allowed to own businesses.

By 1836, 30,000 tonnes of opium were arriving in China each year from India. Jardine Matheson & Company was responsible for a significant proportion.

China attempted to put an end to the drug imports, and raided foreign traders.

In retaliation, the British army attacked the Chinese, killing between 20,000 to 25,000 people, compared to 69 British soldiers who lost their lives.

During this period the Chinese Empire signed what became known as the "unequal treaty".

The Chinese agreed to open five ports to foreign trade and pay 21 million silver dollars to the British government, as compensation for loss of opium earnings and the cost of war.

This 'betrayal' created such turmoil and fury, the civil war

DEAD

that followed resulted in 100 million Chinese deaths.

Decades later, the vacuum left by the end of China's Dynastic rule finally led to the Communist Party coming to power.

To increase the labour force and strengthen army numbers, Mao Zedong encouraged large families and prohibited abortion and the use of contraception.

Mao's strategy led China's population doubling from about 500 million to almost a billion in three decades.

With Mao dead, Deng Xiaoping took to power in 1978. To build economic growth he introduced the one-child policy, to ensure that China's population was restricted to 1.2 billion.

Despite it being originally presented as a temporary measure, China has continued to enforce the strict one-child policy for more than 30 years.

Generations of children have grown up without siblings, or a normal family structure.

A woman's body is the property of the State. The fine for having a second child, as long as it's a boy, is now 10,000 yuan (£1,060). Baby girls are unacceptable.

Women have to report their menstrual cycle to their local family planning monitor, and every three months have a mandatory ultrasound to check their IUD contraceptive device is still in place.

One of the consequences of the one-child policy is female infanticide and sex-selective abortions.

In 2007, in Bobai County in China's south-western Guangxi province, local officials rounded up 17,000 women who were subjected to sterilisations and abortions. They also extracted 7.8 million yuan (£800,000) in fines for illegal births.

One woman, like many others, was eight months pregnant when she was forced to have an abortion.

She witnessed that her baby boy was still alive after the nurse pulled him out from her; the baby clutched to the nurse, who calmly dropped him into a disposal bin.

Other infanticides are often placed in plastic bags and left to float in rivers.

Chinese officials recently declared that 336 million abortions and 196 million sterilisations have been carried out under the one-child policy.

China is one of the few places in the world where if a person dies unmarried, a spouse can be chosen, either a husband or wife, to accompany them after death. This ritual supposedly honours the dead by providing a companion in the afterlife.

Ghost marriages often require a living female to be married to a dead man, sometimes voluntarily but mostly against their will.

She would be forced to live with the family of the deceased, where she endures a life of celibacy.

In other instances, the bodies of deceased men and women are buried together, having never known each other in their lifetimes; their afterlife begins in a marital death-bed.

Consequently in China the trade of grave robbing developed, with a high demand for female corpses.

On average one female corpse is worth $50,000 yuan (£5,285).

There is no remedy in sight for China's rapidly ageing population – one quarter of the elderly live well below the poverty line, and one-third suffer from poor health.

With their elderly population rapidly increasing, especially in Beijing, the younger population is in decline.

With 450,000 elderly living apart from their families, and with about 400 state and private nursing homes, they provide about three beds for every 100 old people in need.

China is admirable in so many ways. However, basic humanity is apparently not one of them.

JUST BEFORE YOU DIE, YOU WILL HEAR MUSIC, FEEL SERENE AND CONTENT.

ACCORDING TO A GALLUP POLL, ABOUT EIGHT million Americans claim to have had an NDE. (Near-Death Experience to you and me.)

Researchers believe the true figure is higher, because people may be uncomfortable discussing the nature of the event with others, particularly if it carries paranormal connotations.

The traits of a classic NDE are:

A sense / awareness of being dead.

A feeling of peace, well-being and painlessness. Positive emotions, but a sense of removal from the world.

An out-of-body sensation – a perception of one's body from an outside position. Sometimes observing doctors and nurses performing medical resuscitation efforts.

A 'tunnel experience'. A sense of moving up, or through, a passageway or staircase.

A rapid movement toward and/or sudden immersion in a powerful light. Communication with the light.

An intense feeling of unconditional love.

DEAD   63

Encountering 'Beings of Light', 'Beings dressed in white', or similar.

The possibility of being reunited with deceased relatives or pets, or religious figures – Jesus Christ for example, in pleasant NDEs, or the devil or demons in distressing NDEs.

Receiving knowledge about one's life and the nature of the universe.

A decision by oneself or others to return to one's body, often accompanied by a reluctance to return.

Hearing music. According to a study conducted by Dr Joel Funk, Psychology professor at Plymouth State College in New Hampshire, close to fifty percent of people who have had a NDE remember an agreeable musical background.

The phenomenon is apparently universal, with the most frequent NDE elements reoccurring cross-culturally.

There are any number of inexplicable examples researchers have reported.

In a Dutch study, a nurse removed the dentures of a heart attack victim who was in a deep coma.

When he unexpectedly awoke, he was able to identify the nurse who had removed his dental work – one of over a dozen who had attended him – and was able to point out the cabinet drawer where the dentures had been placed, despite the fact that the nurse herself had forgotten putting them there.

In a similar study, 344 patients who had been declared clinically dead, with flatline brain stem activity, were able to describe their experiences after being resuscitated.

However, there was a major flaw in the research methodology: patients may have been indeed considered entirely dead,

established by electro-cardiogram records.

But, brain activity had not been measured, and as a result the study failed to establish the exact timing of the experience and how it related to the period of clinical death.

Sceptics therefore believe that the post-death symptoms could have occurred right before or after formal death had been established.

According to Southampton University professor Dr Parnia "death starts when the heart stops beating, but we can intervene and bring people back to life, sometimes even after 3-4 hours, when they are kept very cold".

Others argue that the NDEs of people who are clinically dead are merely psychopathological symptoms caused by a severe malfunction of the brain – the results of the cessation of cerebral blood circulation.

In Theosophy, there are four main regions for the souls of the dead. Kama Loka offers heightened awareness of the karmic event, and the NDE bi-location you inhabit – perhaps leisurely strolling along a lake surface or across a waterfall.

If you are captivated by the subject I can recommend www.near-death.com, which offers a fascinating glimpse into the afterlife, and allows you to share the experience of celebrity NDEs.

Included are Larry Hagman, the main protagonist in the *Dallas* TV series, actress Goldie Hawn, Peter Sellers, Elizabeth Taylor, Sharon Stone, singer Tony Bennett, Burt Reynolds, and creator of *Star Wars* George Lucas.

They also offer convincing examples of people born totally blind, who after being resuscitated from clinical death can miraculously describe the doctors and nurses tending to them, with detailed descriptions of the medical instruments used upon them during their operation.

Children apparently have similar NDEs to adults, and a number of them have accurately foreseen the future.

According to www.near-death.com NDEs can be fully explained by Quantum Physics, sadly not a subject in which most of us feel completely secure.

The site further analyses the differentiations between the NDEs of Hindus, Muslims, Buddhists, Christians, Jews, and atheists.

Helpfully, they also categorise the NDEs of doctors, clergymen, company CEOs, high-ranking soldiers, gay/lesbians etc.

Near-death.com is simply fascinated by the NDEs of people who have attempted suicide, but intervention has saved them.

The site appears to be very proud of its section called 'Debunking the Debunkers'.

It attempts to skewer sceptics who are not convinced by NDEs, who insist that nothing useful is ever brought back, that the existence of God is unlikely, as is any afterlife.

I didn't feel especially debunked after studying their arguments.

The site somehow lost credibility when it went on to recommend "near-death experiences can be produced using a drug called ketamine, which blocks receptors in the brain for the neurotransmitter glutamate".

Not quite the rigourous analytical conclusion that you would perhaps be seeking. (Ketamine is a widely used recreational drug favoured by teenagers at all-night raves.)

WE'RE
ALL·CREMATED
EQUAL,·BUT·IT'S·COOLER
TO·BE·BURIED·THAN·BURNED.

NOW THAT THREE QUARTERS OF US CHOOSE the cremation option, traditional burial has achieved a chic, retro fashionability.

It is simply hipper to be to be dropped six feet below the earth, and a greener, eco-efficient way to be disposed of.

Furthermore, it allows you or your family more latitude in treating your corpse creatively e.g. choice of coffin, location of burial site, tombstone design, inscription etc.

Your favourite outfit can be selected to be worn inside your casket, and some meaningful mementoes can accompany you.

This would be considered part of the healing process for the bereaved; even if nobody is really going to miss you terribly much it will make relatives and friends feel better about themselves, should they be quite unmoved by your demise.

The term 'six feet under' has been used for a television series, the name of a heavy metal band, various songs, and is widely accepted as the standard depth at which to bury a coffin.

During the Great Plague of 1665 London lost 15% of its population, and it was decreed that it would be prudent to bury the infected at a substantial depth.

It was felt this would stop corpses rising to the surface

through soil erosion, and spread the disease once more.

This tradition has continued ever since, although in some parts of the world 18 inches of topsoil above the coffin is considered ample.

Christians bury their dead with their heads at West and their feet at East, mirroring churches, so that the dead will be able to view the coming of Christ on Judgement Day; he is expected to arrive from the East.

Ordained clergy are buried in the opposite position, so that they may rise in the right direction to deliver a sermon to their flock.

Even more vogueish than being either buried or cremated is to be cryogenically frozen.

Deriving from the Greek for 'icy cold', cryonics was first proposed in 1962 as an alternative for those with a dread of death, but with a hearty and determined optimism.

Cryonics is the preservation of the corpse at very low temperatures, with the hope that sometime in the future mankind will be technologically advanced enough to resuscitate the dead, provided the deceased has pre-paid for the procedure.

A central premise of cryonics is that it is possible for memory, personality, and identity to be stored in durable cell structures within the brain that do not require continuous activity to survive.

This is accepted by some medical practitioners, who have observed that patients whose brains have stopped functioning can, after recovery, retain normal memory function.

Cyronics experts also cite the freezing of human eggs as an early indicator of what may be possible in the future.

Cryonics isn't technically classified as an after-death process; scientists argue that whilst the heart has stopped beating, and the person is legally dead (i.e.: nothing more can be done using contemporary medicine), the brain's contents are not

lost, and can be prevented from dissipating if kept virtually frozen, ideally within minutes of the heart's last thump.

In this way the 'dead' person becomes the 'permanent patient'.

In the words of a leading mainstream analyst writing for the American College of Surgeons, "In this era of critical care, death is more a process than an event. A prognosis of death cannot serve as a diagnosis."

When the person is revived they will be regarded as having been unconscious, not dead.

If you are intrigued to examine your options, the pioneers in cryogenics are based in Scottsdale, Arizona at the ALCOR Foundation.

Today, anybody can choose to be cryogenically frozen, if they have deep enough pockets.

Most people pay for their preservation with life insurance, and must take a minimum policy of $200,000 for whole body procedures, or $80,000 for just the head. (ALCOR doesn't like

DEAD

to be thought of as preserving *heads*; they preserve *brains*, and house the heads in tasteful containers for safekeeping.)

All ALCOR members carry a metal necklace or ankle bracelet for emergency use by doctors or paramedics.

It asks for the patient to be given 50,000 mg of Heparin (an anticoagulant) by UV, and that CPR should be used while cooling with icc to 10°c, and keep pH at 7.5.

No embalming/no autopsy and call a toll free number to speak to ALCOR specialists.

Cryogenics operates by vitrifying the organs by adding chemical cryoprotectants to the organs, which can then be cooled to -120°C without forming ice in the body.

Patients are then transferred to large tanks of liquid nitrogen, which each fit four whole-body patients.

ALCOR say that they are improving their techniques all the time, referring to the earlier pre-2000s technology as 'crude'.

Of course the reliability of cryonics is much debated. Arthur Caplan, a director of Bioethics, has stated that the likelihood of a person being revived using these freezing techniques is nil.

If ALCOR manage to disprove him and bring their patients back to life in the future, they offer their clients useful advice.

With no friends or family alive, ALCOR suggest that they try seeking out their descendants.

Caplan argues that we are not programmed for this kind of change, and that furthermore the 'reborn' would have no immunity to advanced infections and diseases.

There are currently 117 patients in ALCOR's facility, and their service appeals to a wide array of people, patiently waiting inside their tanks in Arizona.

Personally, I won't be joining them – my one life appears quite sufficient.

Disneyland
MAY BE THE HAPPIEST
PLACE ON EARTH, BUT IT STILL
KILLS PEOPLE.

ON 11 FEBRUARY 2004, CHILDREN AND PARENTS who had gathered at Disneyland's 'Frontierland' to watch the daily afternoon parade witnessed an unexpected spectacle.

'Pluto' was run over by 'Beauty and the Beast'. Unfortunately, this was not a piece of Disney magic for Javier Cruz, who was inside the Pluto suit.

He caught his foot under the float, was unable to move out of the way in time, and his body was flattened. Cruz's body had to be forklifted out of the parade.

Even if it doesn't cost you your life, taking up a career as a Disney character is not as cheery a role as you would think.

Disney receive about 730 complaints from their cast every year, with almost half of these being costume related.

The weight of the head is the most problematic; the rest of the suit is cumbersome and sweltering in the heat of a Florida summer.

Others have problems with aggressive customers finding it entertaining to hit or push them, leaving sprains, scrapes, and bruises.

DEAD

The costumed 'Tigger' Disney characters have been recorded accosting customers back; one intentionally hitting a child on the head during a photo opportunity, and the other fondling a woman and her daughter as they posed on his knees.

A number of people have lost their lives at Disney parks over the years, mostly due to their own disregard for the safety rules.

But occasionally Disney is guilty of giving the rollercoaster you're riding too extreme a dose of adrenaline.

43 people have died whilst at the four Disney resorts, or later in hospital after an incident.

Some were caused by negligence on Disney's part, some by a rollercoaster rider's medical condition, a variety of accidents, three fatal shootings, and two suicides.

Disneyland America regularly hosts 'Grad Nights' a lethal concoction of drunk undergraduate students and dangerous machinery.

This combination should probably call for extra security and staff at the park.

But Disney thought not, and three young grads have ended up being killed, drunkenly falling out of the monorail onto the track in front of a speeding train.

Others were driving boats while very inebriated, crashing them and drowning.

Despite the fatal loss of three students, Disney still successfully operate their 'Grad Nights'.

One death that did cause Disney to rethink one of their attractions was 18-year-old Deborah Gail Stone in 1974.

She was working as a hostess during her summer holidays on the newly opened 'America Sings' ride.

Once she had greeted patrons and shown them to their seats she stood on a circular stage, the outer ring of which would rotate, taking the audience to the first scene on the carousel.

However Ms Stone stepped too close between the moving and non-moving walls and was crushed to death between them.

Her screams echoed around nearby attractions.

Disney closed the ride for two days, fitted a safety light to let the operator know if someone was too close to the danger zone, and replaced the solid walls with breakaway ones.

It's not only in the Disney parks that disaster strikes; two of Walt Disney's early protégées, child actors Bobby Driscoll and Matthew Garber, whose lives started so promisingly, ended their lives very young and dismally.

Bobby Driscoll was the enchanting boy in *Song of the South* and many other films in the late 1940s and early 1950s.

His natural charm and talent for acting had the industry calling him a 'Wonder Child'.

Sadly Driscoll peaked aged just 16, and embarked on a failed attempt to get more acting work, and became heavily involved with drugs, mainly heroin.

He was too old for Disney, but too associated with Disney for any other studio in Hollywood to want him.

He found a home with other waifs and strays in Andy Warhol's Factory in New York for two years, whilst his drug use spiralled.

Disappearing from the Factory, he was found dead two weeks after his 31st birthday by two boys playing in a deserted tenement, and was buried in an unmarked grave.

His abiding memory for most of us was his role as the voice of Disney's *Peter Pan*, associating him forever with the apt title of 'the boy who never grew up'.

Matthew Garber played cheeky Michael Banks in *Mary Poppins* in 1964.

With his impish air and looks, his London accent and sense of adventure, he encapsulated the ideal Disney boy.

Garber's last cinematic appearance was in 1967, already washed up at age 11. He died 10 years later at 21, having contracted hepatitis in India.

His family denied the suggestion that his hepatitis was related to drugs, and insist he caught it from 'bad meat', which is unheard of medically.

Having built up the Disney Empire to include films, television shows, merchandise, theme parks, and hotels, Walt Disney was still not content.

The plot of land he bought to build Disneyland on in the 1950s was actually much larger than the park.

The surplus bog surrounding it was used to dispose of live alligators that had wandered into the parks and hotels.

Disney somehow managed, somewhat messianically, to create a private Disney government on his land, persuading local officials to give him autonomy over taxes, the roads and public amenities.

In the 1960s, Walt spoke about his true desire – to create a real life utopia, calling it EPCOT or the Experimental Prototype Community of Tomorrow.

His dream for the marsh land next to Disney World died with him in 1966.

In the 1990s, Disney's 'imagineers', as they are called, decided that they would create a town on the land, after realising that it wasn't suitable for park expansion.

They named it 'Celebration', delegated the alligators to a small swamp, and started on their mission to Disneyfy everything they could think of; Walt's sci-fi fantasy was abandoned for a *Stepford Wives* state of perfection.

Celebration is modelled on the small town on Marceline, Missouri where Walt grew up, drawing on nostalgia for a time when life was more homely; neighbourliness, grocery

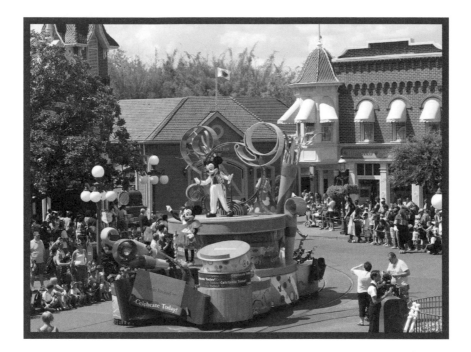

and newspaper deliveries by local youngsters, and babies left outside in their strollers on porches.

30,000 acres of cookie cutter houses make up Celebration, all taking elements of classic all-American idyllic country houses.

The town planners made up a pattern book for the houses, limited to 6 options which all buildings in the town had to abide by.

All houses had to be one of five pastel colours, and the rulebook even meticulously dictated which plants were allowed in the front gardens, and how many houses could have picket fences per street.

People don't move to Celebration to introduce their own aesthetic; they locate there to become part of Disney World.

Celebration is connected directly to Disneyland by World Drive, and unsurprisingly 5,000 Disney fans scrambled for the

DEAD

first 474 homes which went up for sale in a one day lottery event in 1996.

In the town centre, you are endlessly entertained by muzak from the 1940s and 1950s, with speakers hidden in every pristine palm tree.

At the beginning of Autumn leaf-shaped confetti sprays out of the tops of lampposts.

Around Christmas snoap (soap suds which look like snow, in sunny snow-free Florida) is pumped out into the streets, every hour on the hour, accompanied by a constantly cheery Christmas playlist.

Celebration has an unsurprisingly excellent crime record in Florida, with annual robberies of around 3, and just 1 sex offender in every 4,057 residents; in nearby Orlando the rate is 1 in 138.

Until 2010 Celebration kept its admirable clean slate, before experiencing its first homicide, and suicide, in the same week.

This hasn't dented its long-term record as the safest town on Earth.

Walt Disney himself contended with his own personal tragedy which haunted him for much of his life.

Snow White and the Seven Dwarfs was a wildly surprising hit when it was released in 1938.

Hollywood was mystified, as nobody believed it was viable for a feature length cartoon to succeed commercially.

It became the highest ever grossing movie at the time, making $8 million, and still sits at number 10 in the list of the most profitable ever films, adjusted for inflation.

With his new found wealth Disney bought his parents a luxurious home in North Hollywood.

However a defective furnace bothered his mother Flora, who complained of the smell of gas, and within a month of moving in, she died of asphyxiation.

Walt's guilt for having caused his mother's death is said to be the reason for his repertoire of motherless films, most memorably *Bambi*, *Cinderella*, and *Pinocchio*.

ONE HUNDRED
DEAD PEOPLE WERE
WITNESSED WALKING TOGETHER IN INDIA.

LAL BIHARI WAS A CONVENTIONAL 21-YEAR-OLD when he approached his local bank for a loan in 1975.

However he was puzzled to be told that he could not be granted one, not because of a poor credit history, but because he was dead.

In Bihari's native Uttar Pradesh in India, this is not an uncommon occurrence.

The state is the most densely overpopulated in India, with more than 170 million people living on top of each other in a relatively small area.

When a person dies, their property is subdivided between all their heirs, and after decades of divisions and subdivisions, many are left with a plot no bigger than a tennis court to farm on.

This has resulted in fierce conflict between each of the heirs who try and swindle the other beneficiaries out of their rightful share.

The simplest way to do this is by killing off your competition, on paper at least. It is extremely easy to declare someone dead in Uttar Pradesh; you simply visit your local town official and bribe him.

DEAD   79

Payoffs have been transacted for as little as 45 to 2,250 rupees, the equivalent of 50p to £30.

This appears to be a small price to pay for a life.

Bihari's uncle had declared him dead for just £15, and grabbed ownership of Lal's ancestral lands, which measured less than an acre.

Once you have been declared dead, it is bewilderingly irksome trying to prove that you are in fact living.

Judicial delay is common in Uttar Pradesh; with rampant corruption, backlogs, and shortages of judges, people sometimes die waiting to legally prove they are truly alive.

For years Bihari protested his death. Frustrated at the lack of support from officials he took matters into his own hands, turning to extreme measures to prove his existence and get his name onto public record.

He added 'Mritak' to his name, which translates as 'the Late Lal Bihari', tried to get arrested on many occasions by insulting and threatening to murder government officials, and to kidnap his cousins.

He threw pamphlets detailing his case onto the heads of members at meetings of the state assembly, unsuccessfully ran for provincial prime minister, and had his wife apply for a widow's pension.

Ironically, she was denied. The same officials who refused to believe Bihari was alive also refused to allow his widow to benefit from his death.

Finally, after 19 years as a dead man, Bihari was 'resurrected' in 1994, at the age of 40. Receiving letters from many others going through the same plight, he established the Uttar Pradesh Association of Dead People, which now has several hundreds of members in the province.

They regularly gather on protest marches.

It is generally thought that there are tens of thousands of living dead throughout the rest of India.

Undoubtedly in fear that their families may really kill them if they try and appeal their deaths, they remain silent and bear their hardship.

They have every right to feel terrorised. In Uttar Pradesh you can hire an assassin for less than £10, and whilst most Indians are gentle, spiritual people, the same principles do not apply here.

Uttar Pradesh has the highest number of kidnappings, abductions, dowry deaths, and violent crime than any state in India, as well as a vigorous appetite for murder by 'declaration'.

As one of the living dead put it, "it is better to be dead on paper than physically dead".

But the ability to take away someone's life without actually ending it seems nearly as debilitating to the sufferer as a version of Locked-In Syndrome.

With the relentless difficulties that go hand in hand with

being a living-dead person, unable to get a bank account, passport, earn an official living, secure travel permits, or get married, it might be more considerate to do the job properly, although fractionally more of a burden on the conscience.

Lal Bihari was awarded the IG Nobel Peace Prize in 2003 for his 'posthumous' activities. The awards are, of course, a parody of the esteemed Nobel Prizes, and aim to "first make people laugh, then make them think".

Unfortunately not all stories have successful outcomes like Bihari's. One man managed to prove he was alive, but before he had time to move back to his property, his brothers re-registered him as dead.

Uttar Pradesh seems to be so rife with greedy appetites, even the local insects have been influenced.

In one branch of the State Bank of India in 2011, staff were alarmed to find 10 million rupees (£137,000) had gone missing.

Termites had broken into the strongroom and devoured all of it.

This case is not unique; one gentleman lost his life savings after the determined termites worked their way into his bank's 'safe' deposit box.

India's population is the second largest in the world with 1.2 billion residents, one sixth of the world's total population. It is growing so rapidly that India is set to overtake China by 2025.

In a country with such a large and varied demographic, there are bound to be a few irregularities; it is common practice for men to sell off their wives and daughters to settle debts.

Others display their frustration in a somewhat unusual way.

One pair of farmers were so dismayed by their local officials' demands for bribes, they entered their crowded regional tax office and dumped a bag of deadly snakes into its lobby.

Surprisingly, the religion that is practised in India more than anywhere else in the world is the ancient Iranian belief Zoro-astrianism.

Zoroastrians believe that once the last breath has left the body it becomes unclean, the embodiment of all that is evil.

Whereas the earth and each of its elements is godly and pure, disposing of a body by cremation or burial would be seen as polluting nature, contaminating the elements of Fire and Earth, a great sacrilege.

Instead they create 'Towers of Silence', which are a common sight in Mumbai with its thriving population of Zoroastrians.

These tall constructions have flat tops, purpose-built for laying out corpses to be eaten by vultures and other birds of prey.

However, Mumbai's vulture population has been dwindling since the 1980s, due to them feeding on dead cattle who have been administered growth drugs; these have proved poisonous to the birds.

The result is rotting piles of human cadavers being left to rot in the sun on top of the towers.

The hundreds of bodies have to patiently wait for a hungry vulture to descend.

THE·TV·PRESENTER WHO·COMMITTED SUICIDE·WHILE READING·THE ·NEWS·

"IN KEEPING WITH CHANNEL 40'S POLICY OF bringing you the latest in blood and guts, and in living colour, you are going to see another first".

News anchor Christine Chubbuck then placed a revolver behind her right ear and shot herself. Even the TV crew thought it was a prank, using fake blood and firing a blank – until her body stopped twitching and it was clear that she was sincerely dead.

Ms Chubbuck had thoughtfully left on the desk in front of her the script for a third person account of the live suicide to be read by whatever staff member took over the broadcast after the incident.

Morbidly, three weeks before the incident, Chubbuck had asked her producer if she could do a news piece on suicide.

She undertook the research very vigorously, visiting the local sheriff's office to discover the most successful suicide method.

Colleagues reported that Chubbuck had grown frustrated with Channel 40's partiality for sensationalist newscasting, which had increased throughout the 1970s. She deplored the growth of rolling news based television programs filling the schedules, that were to develop into channels devoted entirely to bringing the latest in breaking gory news.

The saying in journalism is that 'if it bleeds it leads'.

DEAD

Recent reporting styles have become no less extreme, as these highlights from recent American news leads demonstrate:

How many sex offenders live in your neighbourhood?

Massive gas line ruptures – could it happen to you? If you think you're immune, you better think again!

What about the water that comes out of your faucet, did you know there is stuff in there that could harm or even kill your kids?

Killer bees! The super bug! The terror threat! The global pandemic! Anarchy! Chaos!

Sensationalism has been the favoured tactic for shock-mongering since the Ancient Romans carved pieces of propaganda, called *Acta Diurna*, and hung them in the forum, like a *Daily Gazette*.

Reporting on everything from the outcomes of trials to announcing marriages and deaths, news quickly spread like Chinese Whispers from those who could read them to those who were illiterate.

In the Middle Ages this power was harnessed to target the lower classes, who having less of an accurate understanding of politics and the economy, could be easily manipulated into believing any news agenda they were being fed.

American politician Budd Dwyer suffered a similar fate to Ms Chubbock, at his own hand a decade later in 1987.

Whilst Dwyer was working as a Republican state treasurer, Pennsylvania discovered that due to state withholding errors, its state workers had been overpaying federal taxes.

Dwyer was charged with accepting a bribe from a California accounting firm, at a time when many companies were offering officials kickbacks to secure the multi-million dollar contract to determine the compensation for each employee. Dwyer faced a maximum sentence of 55 years in prison if proven guilty and a $300,000 fine.

Dwyer maintained that he was innocent throughout the case, but on 18 December 1986 he was found guilty. The day before his sentencing, he called a televised press conference to "provide an update on the situation".

The gathered crowd saw Dwyer read a prepared speech.

"Judge Muir has already told the press that he 'felt invigorated' when I was found guilty, and that he plans to imprison me as a deterrent to other public officials. But it wouldn't be a deterrent because every public official who knows me knows that I am innocent; it wouldn't be a legitimate punishment because I've done nothing wrong.

"The guilty verdict has strengthened my resolve to expose the warts in our legal system. People have said: 'Why bother?' 'No one cares.' 'You'll look foolish.' 'The American Civil Liberties Union and others have been publicising cases like yours for years, and it doesn't bother anyone.'"

Dwyer then paused and handed three of his staffers an envelope each, before pulling a .357 Magnum revolver out of a fourth envelope, and saying "Please leave the room if this will offend you".

Amid gasps from the shocked audience, and cries of "Budd! Budd!" Dwyer called out "Stay away, this thing will hurt someone", then he put the barrel into his mouth and pulled the trigger.

The live footage of the conference showed the whole incident in full close-up.

After his death, the three envelopes were found to contain a suicide note to his wife, an organ donor card, and a letter to newly-inaugurated governor, Robert P. Casey. Whilst Chubbuck's family took the taped footage of the suicide and destroyed it, Dwyer's is available on the internet at www.liveleak.com, for the ghoulish.

Also available on Live Leak is the filmic demise of Ricardo Lopez, who took his obsession with Icelandic singer Björk to new heights, unparalleled by popstar super fans before and since.

Lopez spent his teen years dreaming about becoming a famous artist, and by the age of 18 had become completely reclusive, devoting his attention to fantasising about celebrities.

He settled on Björk, whose artistic non-conformist music and elfin looks appealed to him. His private infatuation eventually manifested itself in the form of a video diary, which Lopez filmed daily from his 21st birthday.

But his obsession wasn't the kind of affectionate lusting teenage girls have for Justin Bieber.

Lopez displayed contempt for the singer, after she started dating fellow musician Goldie.

The 18 hours of harrowing footage document his rapid metal deterioration, as he plans, makes, and sends a bomb from his home in America to Björk in London.

The blast was designed to spray sulphuric acid into the face of Björk, permanently disfiguring or killing her. In his video diary he says he wants to be "the one person who changed her life the most", and calling himself "the Angel of Death". The video tapes were found next to his decomposing body in his squalid apartment, after the stench worried neighbours.

Police quickly alerted Scotland Yard who retrieved the package, disguised as a book from Björk's record label, just before it reached her.

Lopez's final entry shows him at his most bizarre, sitting in front of a hand painted sign saying 'The Best of Me', with Björk playing on the television.

He shaves his head, covers his face first in meat, follows it with paint, then shoots himself. Whilst it was remarkable good fortune that the package never reached its intended recipient, the experience was no doubt horrific for the singer, who took it as a cue to leave London.

She has never returned to her extrovert performing style, which had clearly attracted the wrong type of fan.

YOUR
DEATH MAY
BE VERY POPULAR WITH
YOUR LIFE INSURANCE COMPANY.

YOUR DEMISE COULD BE A HANDY CASH COW for your insurers.

They make great fortunes out of unclaimed payouts from the beneficiaries of life insurance – people who simply didn't know they were the supposed recipients of your money.

The notion that insurance companies go out of their way to track down each potential heir is a romantic myth.

Billions of pounds, dollars, euros remain sitting in their laps, because many of us are unaware that family members, or friends, have left us money – and so never file a claim.

When the law changed in New York State in 2012, it became mandatory for life insurers to make regular searches of their records, to find unclaimed proceeds, and to locate the beneficiaries.

90,000 New Yorkers were suddenly handed a $665 million windfall.

But there is still a $1 billion left uncollected in New York alone.

Following an investigation it was discovered that insurance companies routinely fleece their policyholders, making no

DEAD

effort to honour payments to beneficiaries, and in the worst cases, continue to collect premiums after knowing the policy holder has died.

They just help themselves to the policy's cash reserves until they are exhausted (the funds, not the insurers, they never get tired of holding on to your money).

Of course, insurance companies themselves are routinely the victims of fraud.

In their annual 'Hall of Shame' they highlight some of the more entertaining scams the foolhardily attempted that year.

Inductees are selected from the most brazen, vicious, or laughably inept false claims.

The 'Undead' feature on a regular basis:

Molly and Clayton Daniel dug up the corpse of an elderly woman from a cemetery, dressed it in Mr Daniel's clothes, placed it behind the driving seat of his car, torched it and pushed it over a cliff.

Molly claimed the $110,000 life insurance, with Daniel later returning in full disguise, posing as Molly's new boyfriend.

Unfortunately, too many people recognised Clayton beneath the new wig and moustache, and investigators investigated.

You have to marvel at the blind ambition of Brian Calen, who claimed he lost his eye during a boat cruise.

A Manhattan stock daytrader, Calen explained that the sun filter had fallen off the ship's telescope, and after looking through it, the sight in his sunburnt eye was lost.

After a successful payout for his claim, Mr Calen decided to try the scheme once again, with a new insurance company, and on a cruise once more.

This time, his eye was the victim of an exploding champagne cork scoring a direct hit.

Once more, he received a full payout for his supposed misfortune, so he decided to repeat the idea one more time.

On his third cruise ship vacation, the eye was again injured beyond repair – brutally hit by a flying toy.

His luck ran out when a sharp-eyed insurance fraud specialist determined that Mr Calen's eyes were as sharp as his own, and functioned perfectly.

More grisly was the tale of Tam Vu Pham, who paid more than 5,000 healthy people to allow surgeons to operate on them.

In this way, his Southern California clinic fraudulently billed insurers more than $96 million.

His doctors performed colonoscopies and any number of invasive procedures, before his scheme was unearthed.

Equally heartless was dentist Ahrezi Asgari, who performed hundreds of painful, worthless and botched surgeries on patients – involving root canal work, cavity filling, and extraction.

He earned $370,000 in insurance fees before the elaborate hoax was discovered.

More commonplace is the attempt to claim insurance for 'stolen' property.

Antoinette Millard pretended to be a Saudi princess, and was a regular at New York's fanciest social gatherings.

She was in fact the daughter of a local steel worker, but couldn't afford to continue her charade and tried to raise money by claiming that a thief had stolen $226,000 worth of her jewels.

Her fantasy world had so overtaken her, it never occurred to Ms Millard that anyone might question how she actually owned such giddily expensive jewellery.

Isabel Parker is the 72-year-old queen of the 'slip and fall' scam, throwing herself heavily to the ground in department stores and supermarkets.

She successfully claimed over $500,000 during her long career of 49 tragic falls, before an insurance agent finally connected the tally of coincidences in her accident-prone pastime.

The delightful Carla Patterson tried to win a $300,000 insurance settlement from the Cracker Barrel restaurant in Virginia, after discovering the corpse of a dead mouse in her soup.

But the national chain investigated, and found the mouse had no soup in its lungs, and hadn't been cooked.

Amongst my favourite stories is that of Nicholas Di Puma of Walton, NY, who set fire to his home, and embellished the incident a little further.

According to Di Puma, it all started when two pans on his stove ignited.

After trying to extinguish the inferno with a rag, Di Puma described how he had thrown the first pan out of the window, where it had landed on the back seat of his convertible.

Whilst trying to toss the second pan outside, he tripped in panic and the blazing pan landed on his couch.

He stood helplessly by as both his home and car burnt to the ground.

Unbelievable? Local law enforcement thought so, and he was charged with arson.

The insurance company decided that, under the circumstances, it was probably reasonable to resist paying the insurance claim.

In March 2013 BBC news reported a 'cash for crash' scam run by a 60 strong gang that swindled so much money, car insurance firms raised premiums by a £100 a year.

The 'accidents' involved drivers slamming on their brakes at junctions, hoping the driver behind would crash into them.

The fraudster and his passengers then claimed compensation for whiplash injuries.

They then improved their technique even further to earn

DEAD

more money from the insurance industry by having their associates driving both cars.

The organisation also controlled an auto recovery company which would invoice insurance companies for removing damaged vehicles from crash scenes.

Police believe the scheme netted at least £3 million.

"The criminal gangs organising these operations use the proceeds of insurance theft to fund other serious crime" they said. "Unfortunately this is not an isolated case, and we are currently investigating 49 organised fraud rings across the UK. It is not a victimless crime because everyone's insurance rates rise".

The police's best advice? Don't follow too closely behind a vehicle approaching a road junction.

You may be the target of an accident waiting to happen.

THE·ANSWER·TO POPVLATION·EXPANSION AND·FOOD·SHORTAGES: EAT·CHILDREN·

WHY DON'T WE EAT OTHER PEOPLE? THEY ARE as good a food source as any, and accepted as such by 1,500 cannibalistic species in the animal kingdom.

Scientists have proven that often the most nutritionally beneficial meal a creature can have is one of its own kind, with the added bonus of eliminating competition.

These must have been Jonathan Swift's thoughts when he produced his satirical 1729 pamphlet *A Modest Proposal for Preventing the Children of Poor People From Being a Burden to their Parents or Country, and for Making Them Beneficial to the Publick.*

His alarming mock-treatise suggested ridding Catholic Ireland of its poverty problems by recommending they sell the one-year-old babies of the poor to wealthy English people as a delicacy.

Ireland in the 18th century was in a sorry state, plagued by starvation; the Catholic population were downtrodden after the defeat of James II at the turn of the century.

As with more recent famines, in the Soviet Union, China, and North Korea in the 20th century, cannibalism was turned to as a last resort.

Swift's proposal followed a vogue for social 'reformers' to propose solutions to poverty .

He felt that many of these pronouncements came from men who regarded people as commodities, who believed that keep-

94   DEAD

ing the working classes on low wages encouraged hard work, giving the 18th century motto "people are the riches of a nation" a literal and dehumanising meaning.

His parody read "I have been assured by a very knowing American of my acquaintance in London, that a young healthy child well nursed is, at a year old, a most delicious nourishing and wholesome food, whether stewed, roasted, baked, or boiled; and I make no doubt that it will equally serve in a fricassée, or ragoût".

He doesn't stop with eating babies. "Their skins can be used for admirable ladies' gloves and gentlemen's summer boots".

Swift's satire seems to have inspired a number of people more recently, and it has been seized by the world's artists to embrace his suggestions and test their tastebuds.

Chinese artist Zhu Yu caused outrage with his performance

work *Eating People* in 2000 at the Shanghai Arts Festival. Stealing a foetus from a medical school, Yu prepared and chewed at it, capturing it on film.

People were appalled that Yu, a devout Christian, could consider something so vile.

He argued that "no religion forbids cannibalism" in a Channel 4 documentary *Beijing Swings*, stating that he was merely taking "advantage of the space between morality and the law".

Before Yu was Rick Gibson, a Canadian living in London in the 1980s who realised that the UK has no specific laws against cannibalism.

In fact, people arrested for practising cannibalism are actually charged with murder, but remove murder from the equation, and cannibalism is perfectly legal in our country, and many others across the world.

Gibson had long been dabbling with dead bodies, using freeze-dried ovaries and foetuses to create installations and earrings. But he soon decided to take the plunge into cannibalism when a friend gave him a bottle of human tonsils preserved in alcohol.

Gibson gathered a crowd in Walthamstow Market in July 1988 wearing a sign saying 'Meet a Cannibal'. He sampled some tonsil canapés, becoming the first person to eat human meat in public in British history.

A year later he ate a slice of human testicle he had purchased, but when he tried to re-enact the performance in Vancouver, he was arrested.

But fortunately, cannibalism is a dying art. The only nation where it is still practised it are among the Korowai tribe in Papua New Guinea.

The people they murder and eat are accused of being *khakhua*, or secret witch-doctors. Being animists and deeply involved with the spiritual world, the Korowai pin any misfortune that befalls them as the fault of a *khakhua*.

Sometimes the person murdered is too closely related to the killer for him to eat, so his body is generously gifted to another family.

William Seabrook was an American occultist who spent time with the Guere tribe in West Africa in the 1920s, and wrote about it in *Jungle Ways*.

Despite his keen desire to share in their cannibalistic practices, Seabrook wasn't allowed to partake; he decided to fantasise about his experience, and give it some literary authenticity on his return.

He approached a medical intern at the Sorbonne who stealthily pilfered a buttock of a man freshly killed in an accident.

Seabrook cooked some of the meat in a stew with rice, and roasted the rest.

He reported that "It was like good, fully developed veal... it was not like any other meat I had ever tasted... The steak was slightly tougher than prime veal, a little stringy, but not too tough or stringy to be agreeably edible.

The roast, from which I cut and ate a central slice, was tender, and in colour, texture, smell as well as taste, strengthened my certainty that of all the meats we habitually know, veal is the one meat to which this meat is accurately comparable".

Unfortunately for any in-depth study, most cannibals are often unreliable sources; man-eating men tend to be of questionable mental health, and their reports on the meat are contradictory.

German killer Armin Meiwes insisted human flesh tastes like bitter, strong pork, whilst Japanese cannibal Issei Sagawa said it is like tuna – "tender and soft", and others have debated sweet, sour, tough, tender, fatty, lean.

Experts apparently agree that "this could depend on which bits they have chosen to eat and their chosen cooking method. Some favour the buttocks, and others prefer the heart, upper arm, or palms of the hands".

THE COMPANY THAT THRIVES, DESPITE CUSTOMERS NEVER RETURNING.

SERVICE CORPORATION INTERNATIONAL operates 1,500 outlets in the U.S. very successfully, despite getting no repeat business; not a single client has even come back to revisit any branch.

The company is the world's largest funeral home organisation, as well as owning cemeteries across the nation.

Beginning as a small network of funeral parlours in the Houston area, it went on buying spree to build the brand, buying out its competitors; at its peak in 2000, Service Corporation International owned and operated 3,828 funeral services, plus 525 cemeteries and 198 crematoria, across twenty countries on five continents.

But the market grew stiffer (sorry, more difficult), and for some reason trading conditions led them to re-evaluate, dividing many of their businesses and re-branding others.

In the UK, the company was to now be called 'Dignity', in Australia 'Invocare'.

In a death-defying move they managed to get approval from the Federal Trade Commission to merge with Alderwoods, their nearest competitor in scale.

The FTC blocked their deal initially, citing concerns about consumer choice.

A few more divestments were required, and the buyout sailed through.

In the UK, the market in funeral arrangements is dominated by the Co-op, with 900 funeral homes, but SCI UK brand Dignity is growing faster and hoping to eclipse Co-operative Funeralcare.

The Co-operative were not aided by a disobliging documentary aired on Channel 4 in June 2012.

Staff were secretly filmed storing bodies by stacking them like new washing machines in an industrial estate near a handy motorway.

The warehouse, or 'hub' as it was known, had a fleet of hearses to ferry the deceased to a funeral home should a family wish to see a loved one.

The undercover journalist also witnessed a family being presented with the wrong body, and the correct one whisked over inside a van, the only vehicle available. The reporter saw four coffins being transported by being packed into a glass-sided hearse, with the lids removed to help squeeze all the corpses in.

Also revealed were the hard-sell methods used by staff to encourage expensive funeral packages; that, and the use of 150 industrial scale 'hubs' across the country had enabled profits to exceed £50m annually.

Three months later another documentary on ITV went undercover into a smaller organisation, Funeral Partners, owners of 70 parlours, focusing on six of its branches in South London.

Viewers were distressed that staff showed remarkably little respect for the dead in their care, chanting 'Chelsea scum' at one poor soul before sealing his coffin.

While driving a body in the hearse, staff enjoyed watching pornography on their mobile phones, and embalmers were caught singing sixties hit 'The Stripper' as they removed a corpse's garments, making disparaging remarks about the woman's skin colour.

Clothes bought by families to dress their loved ones were simply stuffed into a plastic carrier bag and put inside the coffin.

In a pep talk to staff as part of a marketing drive, they were encouraged to drum-up business by targeting nursing homes.

They organised weekly bingo sessions, to help solicit business.

The motivation mantra was 'Bingo brings in the bodies'.

I doubt that they would make it to the International Order of the Golden Rule, whose proud membership, by invitation only, comprises of funeral homes 'who are devoted to excellence, quality, and reliability'.

·BUTTERFLIES·
LOOK PRETTY BUT THEIR DIET ISN'T: ROTTING FISH, DUNG AND URINE.

FOR CENTURIES BUTTERFLY SPECIMENS HAVE been collected and taxidermied for their winged beauty.

Most of us would not imagine putting them into the same category as flies, though that is precisely what their name tells us.

Their attractiveness suggests such a species feed only on the nectar of the gods, collecting pollen like bumblebees.

The reality is that butterflies prefer to feed on corpses of fish, decayed fruit, dead carrion, urine, fungi, bird droppings and other animal secretions.

A mystifying natural phenomenon is the annual mass migration of millions of Monarch butterflies from the northern-most states in America, to lower California and Mexico when winter approaches, where the skies and trees are flooded with their orange and black wings.

Like birds, the Monarch butterfly can fly up to 3,000 miles, in an 8-month journey to escape the harsh cold.

During the trip, four generations of the Monarch will have died and been replaced by newborns. Their inborn radar system, which allows them to find their way back to their great grandparents' original home destination, still remains inexplicable.

A more unnatural phenomenon is bee bearding, the art of covering your entire body with bees, that has been practised for centuries.

Mark Biancaniello, an American animal trainer, currently holds the world record for successfully wearing 350,000 bees, which weighed over 87lbs.

In 2009, Li Wenhua and Yan Hongxia, who have kept bees for many years in Northern China, got married whilst both of them were covered from head to toe in a carpet of bees.

A swarm of bees are attracted to their human-beehive by the Queen bee being placed in a small container underneath the chin as bait.

A Queen bee's life is usually a more tempestuous one.

When the Queen bee grows old and her reproductive power diminishes, the male worker bees choose new larvae to feed, one of which will eventually replace the Queen.

The first Queen bee to be born immediately seeks out the other yet-formed Queens, and stings them to death before they emerge, just as the worker bees are killing the old one.

Since all the bees in a colony are born from the same Queen, they are essentially murdering their siblings in order to control the throne.

If you are ever stung by a honeybee, you will know that your revenge is swift; a bee that stings a human dies quickly and grimly.

Unable to pull its barbed stinger back out, it rips off, taking with it part of the bee's abdomen, digestive tract, muscles and nerve endings. The abdominal rupture kills the bee instantly.

Obviously, not all creatures are considerate enough to expire after harming a human.

During the late 19th century, a Bengal tigress became the scourge of Nepal.

She had once been shot by a big-game hunter, and although she escaped, his bullet damaged two of her fangs.

This left her unable to hunt her usual prey, eventually driving her to become a fearsome man-eater, finding us an easy quarry.

Her prolific attacks occurred so regularly and caused such great bloodshed that the inhabitants believed she was a demon, sent as punishment from the gods.

After 200 people had been killed by the tigress the Nepalese government sent the National Army to hunt her down.

But they failed to capture her. She crossed the border to India and it was recorded that she had ended up killing 436 people.

Jim Corbett finally shot her in 1911, and he later became one of the first great advocates of tiger conservation.

But clearly tigers are deadly, as well as magnificent.

Unlike other killers, such as venomous spiders, the tiger remains one of the most beautiful creatures on the planet.

Unfortunately, there are insects that seem gentle and charming, like the dragonfly – but in some parts of the world they grow exceptionally large, and become one of the most brutal predators amongst insects.

A dragonfly can open its jaw as wide as its entire head, allowing them to devour their target, frequently whole butterflies, whilst still in mid air.

To intercept its prey, the dragonfly is able to predict where it will be in the future.

Researchers studying dragonflies discovered that they don't track the object of their appetite, but intercept it, by predicting where their prey is headed, and will get there first and wait for it to arrive.

Dragonflies have powerful serrated jaws, enabling them to mash their meal into an edible pulp.

Although most small dragonflies aren't powerful enough to break human skin, larger ones can and do.

It has been described by recipients as one of the most excruciating bites in the insect kingdom.

DEAD

WHAT WOULD BE THE MOST PAINFUL PART OF YOUR BODY TO TAKE A BULLET?

THERE ARE FEW APPEALING PARTS OF YOUR body to get shot.

Ballistic experts will tell you that people are hit by a bullet in fatal areas, and survive, and others get shot in non-lethal areas, and die.

For example, they point out that over a 10 year period in Chicago's hospitals, 66% of patients treated for gunshot wounds to the head recovered.

If the trajectory of the bullet fails to damage your brain, a deadly-looking bullet wound is often repairable. However brains, unlike hearts, cannot be replaced – nobody has yet invented an artificial brain.

The most fearsomely painful place to have a bullet strike you is the pelvis. The nerve bundles located there effectively distribute pain quickly and excruciatingly throughout the body, often spiraling a victim into fatal shock with the ferocity of the instantaneous agony.

As a bullet enters you, it punctures tissue and bone, crushing

DEAD

or pushing aside anything in its path – creating a cavity thirty times wider than its track.

The cavity closes behind the bullet less than a second after it passes, but the shock waves can damage nearby organs and bones.

Soft tissue can carry the trauma easier than bone; bones themselves tend to splinter and cause further destruction, as their fragments travel through the body as projectiles themselves.

You would be hoping that the bullet flying into you is a 'through-and-through', passing through your body and exiting.

A bullet caught inside you transfers all its kinetic energy to body tissue, ensuring maximum damage.

That is the aim of modern ballistics – jacketed or hollow-point bullets designed to flatten and spread, delivering lethal wounds.

It is generally assumed that the best place to withstand a gunshot are your arms and legs.

Unfortunately, both contain important arteries, and if a bullet severs one of these, loss of blood kills you in a few minutes.

A chest wound will be hazardous even if lands nowhere near the heart – the smashed ribs are going to send bone parts throughout your torso.

Based on their distance from important organs, your hands and feet would be the most welcoming home for a bullet headed your way.

Although it would be an extremely painful experience, because both contain very many bones that would be shattered, a bullet hit would pose the least deadly threat.

The bone fragments are less likely to travel to vital organs, and you will hopefully be blessed with a bullet that passes through your relatively thin hands or feet.

DEAD   107

One bullet wound proved to be a life saver for many.

A poor soul was accidentally shot beneath his left breast bone in 1822, with the musket ball tearing away parts of his left side, exposing bone, tissue, and organs. His stomach was exposed, and doctors simply assumed he would quickly die.

But Dr William Beaumont, a surgeon with a fascination for the working of the digestive system, helped his patient stay alive for 66 more years, though his wound never healed. Beaumont used his exposed stomach to extract digested food, attempting to determine the function of each part of the organ, which up until then had merely been the subject of much theorizing. His discoveries provided a number of life-saving advances in medical research.

I hope this was of some comfort to the unfortunate gentleman whose musket wound provided 66 years of invaluable research.

His body became a hands-on test bed that no laboratory could possibly have matched.

IF·YOU·WANT TO·MURDER YOUR·SPOUSE USE·ARSENIC.

IT'S ODOURLESS, AND TASTELESS. EXTREMELY toxic, you need very little to kill somebody, leaving untraceable amounts lingering in the corpse.

If delivered proficiently the poison is virtually impossible to detect, even for an expert pathologist or indeed the head of CSI.

The mistake most murderers make when they employ arsenic is to overdose the subject of their disaffection.

It then becomes easy to spot, suspicions are aroused, and often a bottle of the poison will be found in the murderer's home or garage or garden.

It's hard to get hold of arsenic, and people are loath to throw it away after a single use, in case it may come in handy in the future.

Untraceable poisons have long been a primary source of fascination within the security services of Russia and the U.S.

And plants have always proved to be a reliable source for a murderer's armoury.

Hemlock grows in Europe and was popular as a poison in Ancient Greece.

Socrates was condemned to death in 399BC, and given a

concentrated infusion; it paralyses the body, leaving your mind fully conscious as your respiratory system shuts down.

Aconite, from the monkshood or wolfsbane plant, leaves only one post-mortem signature – asphyxia. Merely touching the leaves of the plant leads to the poison being easily and rapidly absorbed.

Agrippina murdered her husband Emperor Claudius by mixing aconite onto a plate of mushrooms.

Strychnine is also derived from a plant, but is harder to administer because it tastes unacceptably bitter; it kills by contracting the muscles in the spinal cord, leaving victims in a prolonged, agonizing, and fatal spasm.

Ricin, found in a number of plants, is so virulent and easily distributed it has become a military weapon favoured by despots and terrorists.

It enters the cells in your body and prevents them from producing protein; it is capable of killing large crowds of people who neither need to ingest or inhale the ricin – it is merely absorbed into the skin.

A more recent advance has been the creation of dimethylmercury, a cruelly slow killer.

A dose as low as 0.1ml has proved fatal; however symptoms remain dormant for months after exposure, by which time it is too late for any antidote.

In 1966, a chemistry professor spilled a drop onto her latex-covered hand, and the dimethylmercury passed through the rubber into her system.

Symptoms appeared four months later, but nothing could reverse the poison which took a further six months to kill her.

Polonium, a radioactive poison which is also incurable, recently gained notoriety when used in London on a mysterious Russian, Alexander Litvenko.

Traces were found in his tea cup after the effects of the poison had hospitalised him; the polonium mercifully finished off his tortured body after three weeks.

The track record of our most poisonous fish, insects and snakes ensure they remain the most effective assassins on the planet.

Perhaps the most surprisingly deadly amongst them are the dart frogs that are very abundant in the rainforests.

They are exotically colourful and appealing, but each carries at least 100 different types of toxin in its body.

The more deadly of these, bachrachtoxin and neurotoxin, target the nervous system around the heart, leading to cardiac arrest, coma and death.

The most grisly of our enemies is the Brazilian Wandering Spider, title holder for the record number of human deaths it brings about each year.

Its bite paralyses victims instantly, and men who survive are left with a permanent erection, known as Priapism, until they eventually succumb to respiratory failure.

Anthrax is caused by a spore-forming bacteria that occurs principally in animals.

When passed to humans, what starts off as a heavy flu suddenly escalates, causing most your internal systems to collapse.

Usually victims are people who have an occupational exposure to infected animals, but anthrax has become a weapon of choice for delivery of mass murder.

It is relatively simple and cheap to create anthrax in inhalable form, useful if you want to create terror, or annihilate many people at once.

In America, cyanide is inhaled as a method of execution in prison gas chambers, whereas a high concentrate of potassium chloride is administered for death by lethal injection.

Poison even has its uses in the world of finance.

A 'poison-pill' defence is employed by companies who are wary of being the target of a hostile takeover.

Typically, this involves a scheme whereby existing shareholders will have the right to buy more shares in the company, at a deep discount, if an outsider gathers up a certain percentage of the company's shares.

This effectively dilutes the stake of the predator shareholder, making the cost of the takeover prohibitive.

The potentially hostile bidder would be forced to negotiate with the corporation, and seek approval for an agreed merger.

Poison-pill defences are often controversial, because observers believe they hinder an active market for company shares.

Of course, as in so many aspects of life, the view is different from wherever you are seated.

Investors often buy shares hoping they will soar in value if a takeover bid is forthcoming, allowing them to profit greatly.

For board directors, a stout poison pill defence is considered merely prudent housekeeping.

More prosaically, of course, the poison-pill could be seen as a way for the directors to enrich themselves. The board members routinely seek handsome personal compensation to wave through their consent for the company takeover.

Invented by a mergers and acquisitions lawyer in 1982, a poison-pill strategy has proved as effective a killer of unwanted nuisances as arsenic.

COMEDIANS CAN ALL DIE ON STAGE, SOMETIMES FATALLY.

IT'S TACTLESS PROBABLY TO CELEBRATE, OR even recall, the number of comedians who have died on stage, with the audience thinking it was part of the performance.

In 1987 Dick Shawn fell down during his act and accidentally struck his head on the stage.

He lay there for five minutes until the audience's laughter and giggles slowly evaporated, as they realised it wasn't part of his routine. Shawn was lying on the floor dying.

Earlier, one of Britain's greatest comics Tommy Cooper, adored for getting his magic illusions deliberately and laughably wrong, tumbled to the floor during a performance on a live TV variety show.

Again the theatre and television audience assumed that Cooper's collapse was part of the performance, rather than a lethal heart attack.

Sometimes, fate can be particularly cruel.

Opera singer Richard Versaille was fatally stricken after singing the line "Too bad, you can only live so long".

Gareth Jones was portraying a character who dies of a heart attack during a live TV play. When he died of a genuine heart seizure between scenes, his fellow actors and directors tastefully decided 'the show must go on' and improvised to account for his absence.

Alexander Woollcut also suffered a heart attack during a radio discussion programme with four other individuals.

Listeners were oblivious to the fact that anything was out of the ordinary, other than that Woollcut, known for being strongly opinionated, was unusually quiet.

Film idol Tyrone Power suffered his heart failure while filming a fencing scene in the biblical epic *Solomon and Sheba*. He died after being loaded into an ambulance, and Yul Brynner was brought in to replace him as Solomon.

Another hapless operatic star Leonard Warren expired after singing his aria at the New York Metropolitan Opera. He died before performing his next line "To die is a momentous thing".

You occasionally hear of rock stars being killed by faulty electrical equipment on stage, like Les Harvey, lead guitarist of 'Stone the Crows' murdered by his microphone.

Dramatic, certainly, but not compared to the assassination of

DEAD   115

Brazilian Antario Filho on a live radio show.

Two gunmen burst into the studio, and filled his body with a dozen bullets, in probably the most riveting talk show listeners had ever tuned in to.

The most iconic, and indeed ironic of all theatrical deaths?

Molière, the brilliant 17th century French playwright, who was seized by a violent coughing fit, and died while playing the title role in his play *The Hypochondriac*.

Edith Webster was performing in a musical at a Baltimore theatre in November 1986.

While singing her sentimental finale number, "Please don't talk about me when I'm gone", she suffered a heart attack at the exact moment in the production that her character was meant to collapse and die.

The audience rose to their feet in a standing ovation to applaud her convincing swan song, not grasping just why her death throes were so compellingly authentic.

Several magicians have been felled in the picturesque but perilous act of trying to catch a bullet fired directly at them.

In the 1920s legendary magician H.T. Sartell, the Wizard of the West, employed his wife as his stage assistant, for her to shoot a pistol at him.

The trick involved using soft wax replica bullets, but Sartell didn't realise the deep seated ill-will his wife harboured: she substituted the fake bullets for live rounds at the last moment.

When she gunned her husband down in front of a startled audience, it quickly became clear that his blood-soaked death was not an illusion.

Ralf Bialla was considered a somewhat eccentric German magician, who billed himself The Living Target during the 1970s.

He perfected a speciality act, catching a bullet fired at him across the stage, in his mouth.

His secret was a set of steel dentures, realistically painted to look like pearly white teeth.

In Bialla's dramatic version of the trick, the bullet was fired through three separate sheets of glass, smashing each one as it passed through to reach him.

He held his hands to his lips, clad in steel gloves to form a funnel.

Never making an error, he successfully captured the bullet to display between his teeth, to the amazement of packed theatres.

But sadly the long-term effects of his Living Target act was to give him problems with blood circulation, causing a number of black-outs.

One of these occurred as he was strolling around a scenic mountain pass, and as Bialla admired the views, he passed out over the side of a cliff and perished in the fall.

The Flying Wallendas were renowned across the world for daredevil stunts and circus acts.

When founder Kurt Wallenda stepped out on a wire deployed between the two towers of the Condado Plaza hotel in Puerto Rico in 1978, many news film crews covered the event.

The walk on the tightrope stretched over 100 feet, and 120 feet high.

About halfway across Wallenda was buffeted by a sudden change in wind speed and direction, and fell to his death.

The troupe had always stuck to their code of never employing safety nets.

Leader Kurt always maintained that "Life is on the wire; everything else is just waiting".

DEAD   117

PATIENCE

REALLY IS A VIRTUE ON DEATH ROW.

IN AMERICA, THE AVERAGE DEATH ROW INMATE waits fifteen years between sentencing and execution.

Nearly a quarter of your colleagues on Death Row (who you never meet, you are isolated in a tiny single cell) will die of natural causes while waiting.

Others find a way to commit suicide.

The solitary confinement usually drives inmates, who are presumably mentally unstable in the first place, into such severe madness it would be a kindness to move their execution a little further up the queue.

In 2012 Japan resumed executing criminals after a short-lived 20 month hiatus.

Opponents of the death penalty had cited the example of Sakae Menda, who had been convicted of a double homicide – the murder of a priest and his wife.

He was forced to walk 100 kilometres, barefoot in the snow and consequently suffered severe frostbite.

Then, he was brutally tortured into making a confession.

Thirty-four years later, still held in prison, in 1983 he was exonerated in a retrial.

This was the first successful appeal from death row in Japan.

Today, he is a totem for activists, campaigning against capital punishment.

Another miscarriage often raised is the tale of shepherd Grimaldos Lopez, who disappeared without a trace in Spain in 1910.

Two men, Gregorio Valero and Leon Sanchez, were convicted

of killing the shepherd and sentenced to death after protracted trials, which demonstrated with compelling evidence, the certainty of their guilt.

Just as they were facing execution, shepherd Lopez was discovered alive in a nearby town, to where he had apparently moved, but found just in time to save his supposed murderers.

In 1977, according to Amnesty International, only 16 countries had abolished the death penalty for all crimes.

That figure now stands at 96, with most countries worldwide having revoked state execution in law or practice.

However, 20% of countries maintain a flourishing death penalty system, and these nations represent two thirds of the world population.

Observers in the UK, U.S. and Europe are regularly mystified

DEAD   119

by the inconsistency of sentences passed by the judiciary; many bear little relationship to the relative gravity of the crime committed.

In 2003, George Norris' home was raided by armed police in Texas, who arrived in three large troop vehicles.

After a four-hour long search they loaded 37 boxes of his possessions into the trucks, refusing to disclose to him why he was being targeted for their attentions.

At the time of the raid Norris was 65 years old and an avid collector of orchids.

He later learned that he was suspected of smuggling flowers into America, an offence under the Convention on International Trade in Endangered Species.

Like most of us, although he was an expert on orchids, he had never heard that the blooms were considered an 'endangered species' and that he was therefore an international smuggler.

Five months after the raid he was formally arrested and held in a cell shared with a suspected murderer and two suspected drug-dealers.

They were amused at hearing the reason for his incarceration. One cellmate asked: "What do you do with these things? Smoke 'em?"

George pleaded innocent, but an undercover federal agent had ordered some orchids from him, a few of which arrived without the correct papers.

As a result of the paperwork misdeeds, he was charged with giving a false statement to government officials, and for conspiracy.

Both charges carried the potential risk of up to five years in prison.

Norris ran out of money to continue his defence, and was sentenced to 17 months in jail.

Of course, the great majority of America's prisons are full of

deserving criminals, but with inmates like George Norris it is little wonder that one of every 100 Americans is behind bars.

Lawyers representing death row inmates point out that the "double tragedy of the death penalty in the U.S. is that on review a substantial minority are later found posthumously to be innocent".

Crimes deemed punishable by death vary wildly throughout the world.

To this day accusations of sorcery can lead to torture and death sentences.

In February 2013 a young six-year-old boy died unexpectedly in Papua New Guinea.

His death was unexplained, but a young mother of an eight-month-old baby was accused of causing his murder by using witchcraft.

She was savagely beaten, stripped naked, and doused with

petrol, and burned alive on a rubbish dump by a mob.

In the un-policed towns of South Africa, members heading local communities practise their own version of the death penalty, on those seen as enemies or of having committed a serious crime.

The guilty party is made to stand inside a stack of old car tyres, which are set alight.

This death sentence is known locally as 'necklacing'.

YOUR
FINAL·JOURNEY—IN YOUR·COFFIN,ON THE·NECROPOLIS·RAILWAY.

DURING THE INDUSTRIAL REVOLUTION IN Great Britain, poor living standards and disease meant life expectancy rates were low, and mortality rates were high.

Yet, in the early 19th century the population of London increased from a little under a million people in 1801 to almost two and a half million by 1851.

With its ever-increasing number of citizens the capital was struggling to find room for those both living and dead.

London had a limited amount of burial space, with only 300 acres of land used as graveyards.

Dead bodies regularly had to be exhumed to create room for others; the decaying corpses contaminating water supplies, and between 1848–9 an epidemic of cholera spread across London.

Killing over 14,000, the overwhelming death toll wrecked the burial system of London. To resolve the problem, the Brookwood Cemetery was established by the London Necropolis Company.

Built in Surrey, it was intended to be large enough to house London's deceased. The cemetery was connected to London by railroad, and a station in Waterloo was designed as a fu-

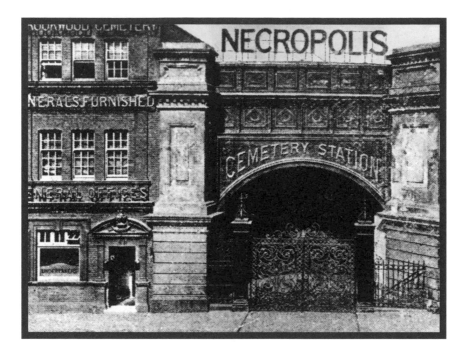

neral parlour for the dead, and for the mourners who were in the waiting line.

The Necropolis Railway meant that dead passengers could be carried aboard, and travel to their final destination.

It wasn't until 1941, when the Necropolis station in London was bombed during an air raid, that it was deemed too inefficient an industry to rebuild, and was consequently closed down.

But in some areas of the world, death is not accepted as your final act, and a journey to a higher plane is anticipated.

On the island of Sulawesi, in Indonesia, newborn infants who die are buried in the trunks of giant trees. The belief is that the child's soul will rise up into the heavens through the great tree, as it grows towards the light.

The burial tree house is a communal resting place to hold the victims of miscarriages and stillbirths, as well as infants who have died.

DEAD

It sanctifies a place for the parents and family of the children to be able to visit, a monument of remembrance for the community.

Unlike many countries in the Western world, this also directly communicates that even an abortion is in reality a death, and should be recognised.

The ritual of burying a dead baby or infant is an integral process to connect with the person who is perhaps most affected: the mother.

In ancient Cambodia the dead were carried up the Cardamom Mountains, to be taken as close to the firmament as possible.

In recent years ten burial sites have been discovered, which have large 'body jars' containing the bones of an unknown Cambodian tribe.

Some bodies were placed 160 feet above the ground on the cliff edges, and the remains date between A.D. 1395 and 1650.

During past centuries, individuals on their journey to the grave weren't traditionally always placed in coffins, or mummified and wrapped in silk, or turned into ashes, or embalmed, or even given a tombstone.

Many hundreds of people have been excavated during the peat-cutting activities in north-western Europe. These are referred to as the 'bog bodies'.

They vary from skeletal remains to astonishingly well-preserved corpses, with their skin, organs, hair, and clothes intact.

The conditions within the bogs – highly acidic water, low temperatures, lack of oxygen – work together to maintain the integrity of the skin and pickle the internal organs.

Physiognomy, even facial expressions, are remarkably lifelike.

Some of the bog bodies brought to the surface date from as early as 8,000 BC, up to the early medieval period.

It is still a mystery how so many people ended up in the bogs,

but it does not appear that they fell into them accidentally.

In the Roman Iron Age, many people in northern Europe were offered up as human sacrifices; others were executed for crimes, or because they were deemed to be cancerous to the social order of society.

Many of the bog bodies that have been found apparently died violent, tortured and ritualised deaths. One unfortunate, found in 1879, was discovered in a bog in Denmark and became known as the Huldremose Woman. Signs on her body show that her arms and legs were hacked repeatedly, with her right arm detached from the rest of her body, before she was deposited in the peat.

Another well-preserved body was that of a 16-year-old girl, discovered in Holland by peat cutters in 1897.

She was found with a woollen band knotted tight around her throat, revealing that she died from strangulation. She was also thought to have been stabbed, the remains of the knife left in her collarbone.

The Haraldskaer Woman, found in earlier in Denmark in 1835 was believed to have been Queen Gunhild, who had supposedly been murdered, and later dropped into the bogs.

Accordingly, her remains were then placed in a magnificent ornately-carved sarcophagus, which was then carried respectfully to the Church of St Nicolai in Vejle.

Some were unconvinced that she was truly of royal blood, and in 1977 carbon testing confirmed this; the body found in the bog predated the period of Queen Gunhild by 1,500 years.

Rather politely, her remains have been left to rest in the Church to this day.

A·HORROR
AIR·CRASH·TO
CHEER·ABOUT.

IN JANUARY 2009 A U.S. AIRWAYS FLIGHT, AN Airbus carrying 155 passengers, took off from New York's LaGuardia Airport.

Flying over the outskirts of the city it struck a flock of birds; they were gobbled up by the aircraft's engines, which both promptly lost all power.

A better man than me, pilot Chesley B. Sullenberger III did not give in to panic.

He decided he must try and get the plane away from the densely populated areas looming everywhere below. Could the airbus possibly drop down into the Hudson River?

Astonishingly, the aircraft glided fairly smoothly across the water, and before it sank, nearby ferry boats, fire boats, tugboats, police boats, converged on the downed plane.

Everyone was rescued safely. Passengers were standing up to their waists or necks in freezing water as the plane began to flood, but nobody suffered more than minor injuries.

A far more horrific aircraft disaster took place in Tenerife in the Canary Islands in 1977, on the airport runway.

Two Boeing 747 passenger airlines collided, with a total of 583 fatalities, the deadliest accident in aviation history.

The tragedy was sparked by a bomb exploding at Gran Canaria airport, targeted by a separatist militia group.

DEAD

The terrorists then informed the security services that they had planted a further bomb, also primed to erupt at the terminal.

The civil aviation authorities understandably closed the airport, directing all flights to Tenerife's Los Rodeos airport – including the KLM and Pan Am aircrafts that were later to calamitously meet up.

Air traffic controllers at the smaller airport were forced to park many aircraft on the taxiway, effectively blocking it.

To compound the difficulties, a dense fog descended on Tenerife, greatly reducing visibility.

With taxiways blocked by parked aircraft, both the Boeings were directed to the only runway available for take-off.

As they manoeuvred into position, the fog grew so thick the aircraft couldn't see each other, nor could the controller in the tower see either plane.

DEAD

With no ground radar at the airport, the only means to identify the location of each plane was via voice reports from the aircraft pilots.

Miscommunication, misunderstandings, mistranslations all conspired to direct the KLM flight to begin its take-off, while the Pan Am airliner was waiting further down the runway.

In the devastating fireball that followed the impact, all 248 KLM passengers were killed instantly, and 335 of the 396 occupants of the Pan Am flight.

Perhaps the confusion was also in part due to the unusual cloud behaviour in Tenerife; clouds at 2,000ft above ground level at the nearby coast, are at 400ft or below at Los Rodeos.

Drifting clouds of different densities cause wildly varying visibility.

The Pan Am aircraft found itself in rapidly deteriorating conditions, with vision reduced to 300ft; meanwhile the KLM flight was in relatively clearer visibility. When it accelerated down the runway, low clouds enveloped the plane, as it hurtled towards the unseen Pan Am aircraft.

Both pilots could see each other's airliner looming quickly towards them, but far too late to avoid disaster.

Runway collisions are rare – but grimly fearsome.

In 1972 two flights collided at O'Hare International in Chicago, then considered to be the world's busiest, and most proficient airport.

A North Central Airlines flight and a Delta Airlines plane collided on the runway, also in foggy conditions.

All the passengers on the North Central flight were killed, but thankfully 93 people on the Delta flight were able to be evacuated from the stricken aircraft.

In Madrid in 1983, a departing Iberia Boeing 727 stuck a DC9, resulting in the deaths of 93 passengers and crew.

At Linate airport in Milan during 2001, a Scandinavian Airlines flight carrying 110 people collided while heading for take off with a small business jet.

All 114 passengers on board both planes were killed, plus four ground workers.

Many seasoned pilots understandably believe their aircraft are often safer in the skies, than they are in airports.

†

Note: Gibraltar airport's runway cuts directly across the busiest street on the island, Winston Churchill Avenue.

Railroad-style crossing gates hold cars back every time a plane lands or departs. The runway traverses the island from one side to the other, built on the only flat space available on Gibraltar.

The landing strip is only 6,000 feet long and requires precision timing from pilots of larger jets.

DEAD   131

Brakes must be fully engaged instantly on touchdown, in order to stop the plane in time. If there is any pilot error, the aircraft would quickly reach the end of the strip, and end up in the sea.

It is a particularly daunting airport even for veteran pilots to depart from or arrive at, particularly during bad weather.

But although it appears to be the most dangerous airport in the world, and comparatively busy for a small island, thankfully there has never been a major accident.

DEAD, BUT ALIVE...

IN 1983, ROM HOUBEN SURVIVED A NEAR FATAL crash and was diagnosed as being in a vegetative state.

Twenty-three years later, using brain imaging scans, doctors reversed the analysis of his condition to 'locked-in syndrome'.

It's hard to imagine a fate more cruel than to be conscious and aware, with no loss of cognitive function, but paralysed so fully, you cannot even blink an eye.

One month suffering such an ordeal is so terrifying a thought, how can we comprehend 23 years of this relentless torture?

There is no standard cure or treatment; however some patients have the ability to move a few facial muscles, most often the eyes or eyelids.

And equally mysteriously, some patients make a partial recovery.

Jean-Dominique Bauby, the man who inspired the film *The Diving Bell and the Butterfly*, was a leading Parisian journalist before he had a stroke which left him left completely paralysed.

Remarkably Bauby learned to communicate using one alphabetic character at a time through blinking – his eyelids being the only muscles he had any control over.

Over the course of two years he dictated his haunting autobiography. But tragically he died of pneumonia only three days after its publication.

Identical effects to 'locked-in syndrome' are created by the poison Curare.

This plant toxin comes from a variety of South American shrubs, and was used by Amazonian tribes as a paralyzing poison which they tipped arrows or blowpipe darts.

Once hit the victim becomes unable to move or breathe, but remains fully conscious and able to feel any torture.

In the 1940s attempts were made by the medical community to use the drug as an anaesthetic, but was abandoned after Frederick Prescott and Scott Smith, two pioneers of the drug, decided to test it on themselves.

Their ensuing terrifying experience of suffocation was enough to prove that Curare does not function as an anaesthetic, nor even an analgesic to counter pain.

Hopefully, the closest we will come to experiencing this kind of paralysis is through a somewhat more psychosomatic effect.

Sleep paralysis has long been documented amongst cultures across the globe; the phenomenon occurs during a shallow state of sleep when the dreamer feels unable to lift a limb or move.

Sleep paralysis is often accompanied by visions and fearfulness. Common hallucinations are of an 'evil' presence nearby, and strangulation.

Doctors are unable to explain this occurrence, but it is believed to take place in disrupted REM sleep, when muscle atonia and weakness have set in.

The presence of an intruder sensed during sleep paralysis seems to resonate with our evolutionary past, a state of readiness to defend ourselves from attack, or run from danger.

Historically, sleep paralysis was thought to be caused by demons or incubi who would sit on the sleeper's chest.

In Scandinavia sleep paralysis is blamed on a mare, essentially the etymology for nightmare, a damned woman whose curse means that she walks in her sleep, and sits on the chests of dozing villagers causing them frightening visions.

Across South-East Asia it is believed that ghosts come to the sleeper and press down on them, sometimes strangling them.

New Guineans hold that it is caused by sacred trees that feed on the essence of humans whilst they sleep. If a person wakes during feeding time they will be paralysed.

In Pakistan it is the fault of a demon named 'Bakhtak', a black magic creation cast by jealous people; children and adults wear amulets to ward off this evil.

The disruption of sleep caused by sleep paralysis is marginal, and no-one is known to have been mortally effected by it.

However there is one strain of sleep deprivation with dire effects on the sufferer.

Fatal Familial Insomnia is rare, but has no known remedy.

The condition involves a continually worsening state of insomnia, leading to hallucinations, delirium, and the eventual shut-down of the major organs.

Caused by a mutated protein, it has been found in a number of families across the world, and is hereditary.

Death usually results between 6 and 36 months from the onset; its development moves from panic attacks, paranoia and phobias, before a complete inability to sleep and rapid loss of weight.

Sleeping pills have been shown to worsen the condition, but very few cases prove to be non-fatal – bringing new meaning to the phrase 'dead tired'.

Sleep deprivation has also been used for centuries as a method of torture.

Not allowing a prisoner to sleep makes them more suggestible, reduces resistance to interrogation, and makes the body less able to resist pain.

Not allowed to rest, the brain becomes increasingly confused, slow to respond, and dreams begin to invade the waking hours resulting in hallucinations and psychosis.

John Schlapobersky was tortured with sleep deprivation in apartheid South Africa in the 1960s.

He wrote: "By the week's end people lose their orientation in place and time – the people you're speaking to become people from your past; a window might become a view of the sea seen in your younger days. To deprive someone of sleep is to tamper with their equilibrium and their sanity."

In the U.S. sleep deprivation was authorised in 2002 in the form of 20 hour interrogations, whereas the military had this extended to 72 hours.

At Guantanamo detainees have been subjected to 'Frequent Flyer' treatment, or 'Operation Sandman'.

One case demonstrated that a detainee was moved cells 112 times during a 14 day period in 2004.

Often prisoners were woken every 15 minutes. Other methods included playing exceptionally loud rap and heavy metal music in the cells, not allowing sleep even to the most exhausted.

The discovery that they also drove inmates to the edge by endlessly playing the theme music from TV's *Sesame Street* prompted songwriter Christopher Cerf, who composed the tunes, to make a film exposing this unusual interrogation method.

WHAT SONG
HAVE YOV SELECTED
FOR YOVR FVNERAL?

PLEASE BEAR IN MIND THAT ONLY 25% OF songs now requested at funerals are hymns.

Only 4% are pieces of classical music.

So if you don't wish to appear fuddy-duddy at your last public appearance, remember to pick something appropriate from this handy list of favourite choices, compiled by funeral homes in the UK and U.S.

1. Frank Sinatra, 'My Way' 2. Sarah Brightman/Andrea Bocelli, 'Time To Say Goodbye' 3. Bette Midler, 'Wind Beneath My Wings' 4. Robbie Williams, 'Angels' 5. Nat King Cole, 'Unforgettable' 6. LeAnn Rimes, 'Amazing Grace' 7. Whitney Houston, 'I Will Always Love You' 8. Louis Armstrong, 'Wonderful World' 9. Judy Garland, 'Somewhere Over The Rainbow' 10. Westlife, 'You Raise Me Up' 11. Celine Dion, 'My Heart Will Go On' 12. Gerry & the Pacemakers, 'You'll Never Walk Alone' 13. Pink Floyd, 'Wish You Were Here' 14. Mariah Carey, 'Hero' 15. Monty Python, 'Always Look on the Bright Side of Life' 16. Vera Lynn, 'We'll Meet Again' 17. Elvis Presley, 'Always On My Mind' 18. Eric Clapton, 'Tears in Heaven' 19. Tina Turner, 'The Best' 20. Righteous Brothers 'Unchained Melody'.

At Finalfling.com you can "capture and update your favourite music on our My Wishes section".

You can add helpful information.

"Explain why you picked the piece of music, who it's dedicated to, or where, when, how you would like it played – live,

DEAD 137

recorded, sing-along, at entry or exit".

They also encourage you to make your own mixed tape of favourites, for loved ones to treasure as a keepsake CD.

"Poignant, painfully beautiful, achingly lovely, soulful, sublime, spiritual, moving, a riot of sound – from soaring violins to sizzling jazz, an Ella Fitzgerald standard, or the Kings of Leon, choose music that makes the heart sing".

If you would prefer something a little less conservative, a musical choice to celebrate your own idiosyncratic charm, the top eight most popular, but more unusual, requests last year were:

1. Queen, 'The Show Must Go On' 2. AC/DC, 'Highway To Hell' 3. Queen, 'Another One Bites the Dust' 4. Bon Jovi, 'I'll Sleep When I'm Dead' 5. The Wizard of Oz, 'Ding Dong the Witch is Dead' 6. Willie Nelson, 'Hit the Road Jack' 7. Right Said Fred, 'I'm Too Sexy' 8. INXS, 'Never Tear Us Apart'

Funeral directors were surveyed by the website 'Your Tribute' and believe that the new preference for pop music to accompany a demise is part of the Princess Di effect; 'Candle In The Wind' was sung live at her funeral by Elton John, to welling eyes around the world.

Surprisingly popular at German funerals are Avril Lavigne, with 'When You're Gone', at 3; Enya at 2 with 'Only Time'; and the list also features, rather oddly, Christina Aguilera's 'Hurt'.

In Australia they like Mariah Carey's 'Hero', Barbra Streisand's 'Memories', Bill Withers' 'Lean On Me', Bob Dylan's 'Forever Young', Cat Stevens' 'Morning Has Broken', Guns N' Roses' 'Knockin' On Heaven's Door'.

In Holland the number one choice is an English song, Katie Melua's 'Cried For You', with Dutch hits filling the next top spots.

Before you select your personal farewell favourite, bear in

mind a quarter of funeral homes keep a blacklist of songs banned at services.

They include The Trammps' 'Disco Inferno' ("*burn baby burn*"), and John Lennon's 'Imagine' ("*imagine there's no heaven*").

Please try and restrain yourself from TV show theme tunes.

Even I would be embarrassed to pick the opening bars of *Dr Who*, *Match of the Day*, *The Muppet Show*, *Top Gear*, *The X Files*, or *Six Feet Under*, all of which are currently leaving more conventional funeral melodies in their wake.

As well as recommending funeral tunes, Your Tribute's Permanent Online Memorial service offers to commemorate the lives of lost loved ones, eternally.

"Create free online obituaries or premium memorial websites for loved ones in minutes.

Invite friends and family to share their condolences, stories, memories, photos and videos on the memorial.

Easily integrated with all social media websites, the memorial is completely customisable with designer themes, life stories, guest book, and gifts, and is available online for free, for life, we guarantee it!"

Whose life they refer to remains unclear.

The memorial page will include "tasteful, well-targeted banner ads" discreetly flashing, unless you are prepared to pay for the "very reasonably priced premium package".

†

Note: The flowers alone at Reverend Sun Myung Moon's funeral in September 2012 in Seoul cost £250,000.

Moon, founder of the Unification Church, disliked his flock being described as Moonies, preferring the term 'Unificationists'.

He died at 92, after setting up his church in refugee camps in South Korea in the 1950s. He claimed that he regularly

conversed with Jesus, and both he and his followers believed that he was an incarnation of God.

His church is extremely well endowed, owning newspapers including *The Washington Times* in the USA, arms factories in South Korea, food distribution enterprises, as well as universities around the world.

350,000 mourners attended his funeral.

THE ETERNAL QUESTION. WHAT TO DO WITH YOUR ASHES?

YOUR CORPSE CAN HAVE A MORE INTERESTING afterlife than merely being left in an urn in someone's sideboard.

Celestis Memorial Spaceflights specialises in shooting ashes into the heavens aboard a spaceship.

Their service was inaugurated in 1999 at the request of NASA when Celestis assisted the colleagues and loved ones of the planetary scientist Dr Eugene Shoemaker in placing his cremated remains aboard the Lunar Prospector mission.

They explain that a reservation can be made on a preferred or particular flight, at a premium charge; otherwise, ashes are simply placed in the next available lunar launch.

The basic package costs $12,500, but they can include two cremated remains for only 50% excess.

The most celebrated ashes launched into space belong to Gene Roddenberry, creator of *Star Trek*.

Alternatively, your friends and relatives may wish to have your ashes mixed with ink and tattooed into their skin.

Tattoo artist Shane Dyson explains "losing a loved one is always traumatic and if I can do something to help with that it's really cool".

There is the additional dubious pleasure of knowing that you will be getting forever under their skin.

Some medical practitioners have concerns that the ashes may not be sterile, and there is a chance that they could cause an infection, or that there "may be an allergic reaction to a foreign body" (sic) "being placed beneath the skin's surface".

LifeGem can offer to take cremated ashes and turn them into "certified high-quality diamonds, a way to embrace your loved one's memory day by day. And of course we have a full line of cremation jewellery, rings, and pendants to accent your beautiful LifeGem cremation diamond".

They offer a range of colour options for you: white, blue, red, yellow, or green LifeGems are available.

Another colourful memento can be found at Scattering Ashes.co.uk, who offer a collection of fireworks each containing some of your ashes, to make for a remarkable display.

It costs £75 per rocket (minimum four rockets per order). They "are made to a design by a pyrotechnic expert" and by "firework professionals who show the utmost concern and respect".

The Good Funeral Guide is a fine source for helpful guidelines on, as they put it, "what to do with the ashes".

They point out that Rolling Stone Keith Richards snorted his father's remains, that rapper Tupac's band members the Outlawz rolled up and smoked his ashes, and that a lady called Denise Moon took the ashes of her late partner to court to prove that she was not evading Council Tax.

They worry that "a favourite way with ashes is to scatter them at a sight which the dead person loved, but there are drawbacks; if it's a popular beauty spot you may feel inhibited by the proximity of other people. You won't have a good experience if you wait anxiously until no one's looking and do it surreptitiously".

So many people do this at Jane Austen's cottage apparently, that "fly-tipped remains have become an unsightly nuisance".

And they warn that football grounds will not let you spread ashes on the pitch.

They offer eco-friendly urns in papier-mâché handmade designs, and suggest scattering ashes from a hot air balloon, or at sea.

They also helpfully point out that you can get ashes pressed into a vinyl record to play a favourite piece of music from Andvinyly.com. Their slogan? 'Live on from beyond the groove'.

You will find a marvelous section on the Good Funeral Guide, 'Do It All Yourself', where you conduct a home-based funeral.

Invaluable advice is offered:

"*When someone dies, most public officials advise you on the assumption that you will want to use a funeral director. Some will express amazement that you want to do it all yourself, some may try to dissuade you, some will disapprove and some will try to stand in your way.*

If anyone tries to tell you it's against the law, put them right. It's not. Tell them you are the funeral director.

If you feel strongly about letting strangers take your dead person away to do with them you know not what; if you feel strongly that it's your duty to care for them and spend time with them in death as in life; if you think you have the emotional and physical strength to enable you to do that, then you may well be prepared and equipped for the task.

DEAD   143

It needs serious thought. Not only can it be difficult in itself, it may also be difficult to explain to friends and neighbours. It's an unconventional thing to do.

What will your close family members and friends think? You will need their help. At least four of them, preferably six.

Before you can sensibly undertake any practical task in which you are unversed, you need five things: an understanding of the difficulties; an understanding of the worst that can go wrong; the right equipment; our workshop manual; the phone number of an expert who can advise – or ride to your rescue in case of calamity.

If the person has died of a disease which would put you at risk from infection, your doctor will tell you.

Most viruses and diseases can survive no longer than a few hours in a dead body. The microorganisms associated with decomposition are not the kind that cause disease. Smells don't kill.

Almost all dead bodies are not dangerous. Gloves and simple protective clothing are all you need – and a mask, if you like.

In most cases, if you keep your dead person at home for no longer than a week, so long as you keep him or her cool all should be well."

According to Erika Nelson, a funeral director, quoted in the Crossings Manual for Home Funeral Care, the following conditions make a body especially difficult to care for: bed sores – open wounds which leak fluid; oedema and fluid-filled blisters; obesity; certain infections; septicaemia; rapid decomposition.

This may be hastened because of the duration of the dying process; the cause of death; the size of the body; the contents of the stomach; and the presence of medication (especially cancer drugs).

Ms Nelson adds:

"A nurse may be able to offer an opinion, as sometimes, decomposition can progress very fast.

You'll need a coffin, which you can either make yourself or buy.

You will need strong and willing hands to help you."

The gentleman whose last wish I much admire was Fredric J. Baur, inventor of Pringles Crisps. His family agreed to lay his ashes to rest, as he had requested, inside an empty, original flavour Pringles can.

Incidentally, if you didn't already know, human ashes are known as 'cremains' in the trade.

DEATH·DEFYING STUNTS·THAT DIDN'T·DEFY·DEATH.

IN APRIL 2013, INDIAN DAREDEVIL, AND GUINNESS World Record holder Sailendra Nath Roy decided to take on the challenge of beating his own title.

His achievement was to have travelled the longest distance suspended by zip wire attached by only his hair. His long locks, shaved around the sides with a lengthy ponytail at the crown, proved the perfect style for the task.

Police driver by day, Roy was daring enough to extend his record of 82 metres, set at the Neemrana Fort Palace in India, by covering a distance of 183 metres lifted by his hair 21 metres above ground.

As he set off from one side of the void, he seemed to be on track to achieve his goal.

About halfway, he became entangled and struggled to move. Trying to call out for help for 30 minutes, he eventually grew still, having suffered from a severe heart seizure.

It was a further 15 minutes before people were able to bring his lifeless body down.

Over a thousand people witnessed his harrowing demise, and though captured on multiple cameras, it is impossible to determine which of the later pictures were pre- or post-mortem.

Joseph Burrus was an American businessman who enjoyed himself being a local entertainer.

For Halloween in 1990, the Blackbeard Family Fun Centre decided to produce an event to raise money for a local drug rehabilitation centre.

Burrus, himself a recovering addict, volunteered to perform his 'failsafe' coffin escape, using his epithet 'Amazing Joe'.

Proclaiming to be the next, even greater, Houdini, Burrus had created a transparent plastic coffin – he would enter it, chained up, and buried under soil, topped with quick-drying wet cement.

Clearly he felt his magic skills would prevail, despite local radio stations, his wife, children, friends, and colleagues telling him his plan carried too high a risk of death. Apparently, his above ground trials did not produce a comforting success rate.

Nonetheless Burrus was determined, and all of his family, plus a large audience and many journalists armed with video cameras were there to witness every moment of his great escape.

The notion was for Burrus to free himself from his chains, and exit out of the box after the cement was poured on top. He would be able to burrow his way up, out of the still wet cement, before it set solid.

He had, in fact, previously performed a similar act, one that Houdini had never perfected, buried inside a sturdy wooden box with soil placed on top of him.

Burrus was in his coffin being lowered into the ground when he frantically halted proceedings, claiming that the chains around his neck were choking him.

Loosened slightly, and momentum lagging, he was placed in to his 7 foot deep grave and was covered, as instructed, first in 3 feet of soil, then under 6,000 pounds of wet concrete.

Seconds after they had finished smoothing the surface, it all suddenly collapsed, sinking horrifyingly fast, as the concrete caved in, crushing the flimsy coffin.

Struggling to get to Burrus as quickly as they could, the panic-stricken crowd started digging out chunks of cement with their hands.

When they reached him it was clear that a recovery was impossible, and that he had perished, buried alive.

Speaking in an interview after his death, Burrus' assistant said that she had expressed fears about the act to the illusionist, reminding him that there was no scientific research to prove that the handmade coffin could withstand the weight of the soil and concrete.

Burrus had simply tested his contraption by jumping on it – and he quoted Houdini as his response: "It will either be fate or my foolishness that kills me".

Matt Cranch, the 'Human Cannonball', died in front of bank holiday crowds in a Kent showground in April 2011.

Dying doing what his friends claimed he loved most, Cranch was fired 50 feet into the air by a giant cannon. The net that was meant to catch him failed to do its work.

More than thirty human cannonballers have died around the world during the performance of this epic stunt.

Some have been ejected at over 70mph, and flown about 200 feet.

Amongst those who take the comparatively stable job of being a movie stuntman, many lives also end grimly, despite the best planning, equipment, and experts always on hand.

In 2004, movie fans giggled ironically when Brad Pitt tore his left Achilles tendon, whilst playing Achilles in *Troy*.

The film's producers failed to reveal that a bodybuilder had actually died on set, after severe complications from a broken leg.

In 2002, Vin Diesel's stunt double, Harry L. O'Connor, was killed during a scene in which he was supposed to fly down a parasailing line and land on a submarine.

However he struck a bridge at high speed and was killed instantly.

Bruce Lee's son Brandon followed his father's career path, performing his own stunts, but unfortunately died during the filming of *The Crow* in 1994, when a co-star shot him with a gun that was supposed to be filled with blanks; accidentally, it contained a real bullet.

In 1991 stuntman Jay C. Currin was killed on the first day of filming *Bikini Island* when he dived off a 55 foot cliff and the airbag he was meant to be landing on had not been positioned correctly. Instead he threw himself headlong onto rocks.

American escapologist Rick Maisel should by all accounts be dead, but he keeps defying it.

Maisel invented a spectacle to captivate his audience, the 'Washing Machine Escape'. Maisel always dreamed of being a master magician, quickly tiring of familiar routines.

He had the idea of incorporating washing machines into his act, and after much practice, he learned to control the vomiting reaction that all of us would endure when hurled around in inside a violently rotating machine, for 30 minutes of 1,600 full revolutions.

Bound with handcuffs and leg irons, he climbs into the washing machine, which needs to have at least a 24 inch drum and 12 inch door, and has an assistant press 'start'.

He doesn't hold back on the washing powder either, and has to withstand the soap being tossed wildly at him.

The average cycle does 50 or 60 revolutions per minute before going into the deadly spin cycle of 450 revolutions per minute, which should kill the man inside in 3 to 5 seconds. Unable to hold his breath in the machine, as the bubbles are forced into his nose and mouth, Maisel spits out soapy water calmly without hyperventilating.

His talent for endurance has taken him around the world, on to countless television shows and theatres. He has perfected his skill inside 50 different makes of washing machine, selected at random for him to demonstrate the performance is not a fix. Terrified audiences watch him being tossed ferociously around for about 15 minutes.

Maisel uses self-hypnosis and was taught transcendental meditation by a Maharishi at age 15, and trained to be able to lower his heart rate on command. This allows his body to require less oxygen when inside the machine.

He also enjoys performing the 'safe escape', which is far from safe; it involves finding a way out from inside a high-tech unbreachable safe, supplied untouched direct from the manufacturer.

Inside there is a limited 3 minute air supply.

Rick is still performing.

THE DEATH CLOCK.

THERE ARE A NUMBER OF INTERNET SITES THAT can tell you how many days you have left to live.

You answer a few simple questions, and voilà, you can effectively start forward-planning funeral arrangements.

Not surprisingly you will be quizzed about your age, family genetic history, diet, exercise, alcohol consumption, smoking, risky pastimes, the life span of your parents, health problems amongst siblings.

They want to know the scale of your unprotected sex with different partners – never, rarely, sometimes, often, very often.

Curiously, they are also fascinated by how regularly you floss your teeth, from three times a day, rarely, or never.

The amount of time you spend in the sun also forms part of their calculations: none, very little, moderate amounts, quite a lot, all the time.

Drug use is a factor, and I don't think they are referring to headache tablets.

They ask how often you share needles during drug usage, your choices being: I say No to drugs, very rarely, sometimes, often, very often.

How regularly do you eat processed meat or poultry, how regularly do you use butter and cream, how much coffee do you drink a day, how much of your diet is non-vegetarian, how do you like your fish and meat cooked?

Are you exposed to air pollution? Are you in a high risk area for Radon exposure? Do you use a two-wheeler or a four-wheeler?

How often do you find yourself stressed – very rarely, very often, occasionally?

Puzzlingly, you are not given the option to claim you are never, ever stressed.

They are interested in whether you are pessimistic, optimistic, sadistic (?), or normal (?).

Are you over your physician's recommended weight? Are you underweight, optimal weight, 15lbs overweight, 30lbs, 80lbs, or more?

At this stage on your quest for an accurate forecast of your doom, the site gets down to business.

It offers you the perfect 'lucky stone' to wear, precisely selected for you, for $10.

They will, for a fee, unlock the secret of the five foods you must never eat.

Similarly they can offer a personal astrology reading, at a reasonable fee, and palm readings via scanning your hand's ink impression that you send to them.

You may take your pick from Indian or Chinese or Tibetan horoscope readings.

At www.FindYourFate.com you are also offered love tips, lessons on how to kiss employing a variety of styles, love poems for you to employ on Valentine's Day, and a wide choice of love tokens and gifts to select from.

Also available are Death Clock shirts, Death Clock screen-savers, iTunes mobile horoscopes, a guide to becoming a fashion model, a full matchmaking service, and dream analysis.

They recommend compatibility readings before you enter into a commitment.

They even offer a name-changing service: "Finding a suitable name is a complicated process and involves esoteric calculations. We employ persons of proven calibre who will provide you with the best of services and help you realize your potential".

They can also provide an astrological profile for your pet cat or dog.

I'm sure you will find your visit to the site fulfilling.

At www.DeathClock.com their slogan says "you can conquer the most perplexing uncertainty in life: your death. Then, rest in peace…"

KILLED BY TUTANKHAMUN'S CURSE? OR A PSYCHOPATHIC SATANIST?

MORE THAN TWENTY PEOPLE INVOLVED IN the opening of King Tutankhamun's burial site at Luxor, Egypt, in 1923 were subsequently found dead in gruesome circumstances.

For years, the public blamed the 'Curse of Tutankhamun' and the supernatural powers he could still command from his burial chamber.

But the mysterious deaths had a more prosaic, though equally grisly, explanation.

They are believed to be the work of a notorious satanist Aleister Crowley, who masterminded a series of ritualistic killings in a delusional frenzy of retribution.

Crowley held archaeologists Howard Carter and Lord Carnarvon responsible for opening the tomb, and decided to destroy anybody associated with supporting "the desecration of the Boy-King".

Writer Mark Benyon, 'in the light of new evidence', holds that Crowley, who was also obsessed with Jack the Ripper, engineered a series of murders to avenge his totemic leader, Tut.

These included Captain Richard Bethell, smothered at his Mayfair Club

Lord Westbury, flung from a seven storey building in London.

Sir Ernest Budge, killed mysteriously when keeper of Antiquities at the British Museum.

Ali Kamel Bey, a young Egyptian prince, was shot dead by his wife Marie-Marguerite shortly after visiting King Tut's tomb.

It appears that Crowley was her lover, and incited her to carry out the shooting.

Mark Beynon may be fanciful in some of his suppositions, but he has sold many books of the back of these theories.

Benyon bases his accusations on the fact that Crowley had derived the basis of his occult religion, Thelema, from ancient Egypt sources; indeed *The Book of Law*, the bible of the religion, was said to have been delivered to him by the Holy Guardian Angel, Aiwass, during a stay in Egypt in 1904.

However bizarre and deadly Crowley's activities may have been, and despite a desire for much satanist sexual proclivity, he was a devoted father, and tried desperately to support his wife, who battled alcoholism throughout her life.

Resorting to a systematic scheme of murders could appear somewhat far-fetched, even if Crowley did tend towards sacrifices of animals, and frequent blood drinking.

He certainly faked his own death. The latter performance took place in Portugal with the help of poet Fernando Pessoa.

The 'death', occurred at the Mouth of Hell, a formation of rocks famous for the fury the of waves that blasted a chasm through the stone.

Crowley greatly enjoyed reading newspaper accounts of his death, and then reappeared three weeks later in Berlin.

Crowley was born to a rich family who had made their money in brewing, and he went on to study philosophy at Cambridge.

A keen mountaineer, he spent much of his youth climbing

the French Alps and even attempted to climb K2 – snow blindness and flu ending this expedition.

At Cambridge he had a particularly active sexual life, picking up girls in the surrounding pubs, and selecting a variety of prostitutes.

Eventually he embarked on homosexual affairs, and the freedom of sexual experience was to remain a key tenet of his particular brand of religious occultism, that he summarised as 'do what thou wilt'.

After university he became a member of the Golden Dawn order and moved to London where he developed his 'skills' in ceremonial magic and alchemy.

He eventually married, and honeymooning with his wife Rose he travelled to Egypt, where he became obsessed with the God Horus.

His wife was similarly possessed during this time and took him to the Stele of Ankh-ef-en-Khonsu, the museum exhibit number for which was 666.

Newly re-naming his wife 'Ouarda the Seeress' he devoted his time to writing *The Book of Law* and declared himself a prophet of a new age of mankind.

In his book, *Secret Agent 666: Alesteir Crowley, British Intelligence and the Occult*, Richard Spence puts forward a case for Crowley having being an active agent for British Intelligence throughout his life.

He travelled a great deal, through Mexico, Asia and North Africa, and lived in America for a time.

He also published writings in German magazines.

In the book Spence proposes the notion that Crowley would have been strongly placed to gather information on German intelligence networks and the Irish independence movement.

He cites a document from the U.S. Army's Military Intel-

ligence Division – "Aleister Crowley was an employee of the British Government... in this country on official business of which the British Consul, New York City has full cognizance".

He died at 72 of a respiratory disease brought on by heroin, to which he had become addicted after being prescribed morphine for asthma and bronchitis.

His grip on the imagination of successive generations has remained a powerful one.

In 1970 Led Zepplin guitarist Jimmy Page purchased Crowley's old house which stood on the shores of the Loch Ness.

Boleskeine House was desirable as the ideal location to perform certain spiritual rituals that demanded a north-facing window, and various other architectural specifics.

Page owned the house for a decade and claimed that it was haunted by a severed head.

DEAD 157

Crowley would be amused that after all these decades, recent fans include rapper Jay-Z, whose clothing line currently bears the 'do what thou wilt' on it.

Or he may consider someone like Paris Hilton wearing a T-shirt sporting the letters 'OTO' – the Ordo Templi Orientis, the name of the secret society Crowley was leader of – a rather inauspicious end for his legacy.

THE·ULTIMATE REVENGE. MURDER·YOUR MURDERER.

THE HUNGRY SNAKE SEEN HERE MADE A FATAL
error when he decided to make this tarantula his lunch.

Fatal indeed, because as he digested the spider, the tarantula's toxic venom was released, paralyzing and killing the
Carpet Python.

Of course in most cases the murdered are incapable of exacting
revenge on their killer.

In fact, there is more discomfort in knowing that many murderers complete their jail sentence for a brutal slaying – and
upon release promptly kill again.

Do you believe some people are born with an inbuilt capacity for slaughter? I am not referring to serial killers, psycho-
paths who simply draw pleasure from killing numerous people
during their career path.

John McRae of Florida was a paedophile sentenced to a Life
Term for stabbing an 8-year-old boy to death.

Released in 1971 after serving 20 years, he was later convicted of another child murder, with further counts pending.

John Miller of California killed an infant in 1957 and was
convicted, released on parole 17 years later and quickly murdered his parents, landing himself another life term.

Timothy Buss murdered a 4-year-old girl, and was sentenced
to 25 years in 1981. Paroled 12 years later he murdered a

DEAD   159

10-year-old boy, and was jailed again in 1996.

Arthur Shawcross was released after serving 25 years for a child murder, and then turned to killing prostitutes, at least ten in all.

Howard Allen killed an elderly woman and was sentenced to 21 years, but released after 10. He then beat an 87-year-old woman to death, and followed that up with slaying another 80-year-old.

He was jailed once more after his conviction.

The lengthy list of similar cases is bewildering.

This has empowered a group of activists who are seeking a return to the death sentence as the norm across America; they believe there is ample evidence to demonstrate that the fear of the death penalty deters murderers. Not as vocal as the anti-state-execution groups, they point out that capital punishment is an unarguable way of saving lives.

During the temporary suspension of the death penalty in the U.S. between 1972 and 1976, the murder rate doubled.

But throughout time, there have been victims who felt themselves unsatisfied with official punishments, and were driven to take the law into their own hands.

The Nakam were groups of Jewish assassins that targeted Nazi war criminals with the ambitious aim of avenging the Holocaust after the end of WWII.

Meaning 'Avengers' in Hebrew, the Nakam had a specialized Executioner Unit of around 60 trained killers who wore British uniforms, and set about arresting Nazis, giving them summary trials to ensure they had been directly involved in killing Jews, before murdering them.

After the extent of the horrors at Auschwitz, Buchenwald, Dachau and the other Nazi death camps were made public, the Nakam sought mass revenge. They moved on from

shooting and strangling their oppressors directly, one-on-one.

They turned to poisoning water and food supplies. In 1946, 1,900 German prisoners of war in a U.S. camp were poisoned through arsenic-laced bread, although only around 400 Germans died from the effects.

They felt no compassion for those they killed, much like the rest of the Allied forces at the time, who had lost so many comrades in the war.

Vengeance even on a dramatic scale didn't give the Nakam the recognition they desired, in order to grow the movement; their activities were drowned by other postwar stories.

Of course, the public's attention has always been ignited by the details of gruesome murders, and tales of blood-soaked revenge.

Anthony Stockelman, 39, molested and took the life of 10-year-old Katie Collman and was easily caught; his DNA was found on her body and on a cigarette butt found nearby the crime scene.

He was serving a life sentence in an Indiana prison in 2006, a hardline correctional facility without sufficient checks in place to realise that Katie's cousin was incarcerated in the same jail.

One night Stockelman was ambushed by inmates and now bears permanently, on his forehead and across his face in deeply scored capital letters, 'Katie's Revenge'.

Lorena Bobbitt had the most publicised case of vengeance in recent history.

Her husband John Bobbitt often came home drunk and violent and would force himself on Lorena when she was sleeping.

However one evening she had had enough. When he had fallen asleep, in a whirlwind of rage that she recalls as a blur, Lorena grabbed an eight inch long kitchen knife and chopped off his penis.

Jumping into the car and driving, penis in one hand, knife in the other, Lorena suddenly emerged from her stupor and realising she didn't have proper control of the wheel, flung her prize out of the window.

As she came to her senses and realised what she had done, she called the Emergency Services in a panic.

Although the chance appeared slim, they managed to find Bobbitt's penis in the grass and rushed both it, packed in ice, and its owner to the hospital, while he was rapidly losing blood.

After nine and a half hours of delicate surgery, John's penis was reattached; he was warned he might never be able to have sex again and used a catheter for two months.

Lorena's trial plea in court of temporary insanity, and that the attack was not pre-meditated but in self defence, swayed the jury who eventually found her not guilty. Bobbitt too was found not guilty of abuse and freed due to lack of evidence.

In the years following, Lorena disappeared, while John took advantage of his new position as 'most famous owner of a mutilated penis'.

He capitalised on his story by going on endless chat shows, forming a band called The Severed Parts, having a penis enlargement operation, and starring in two porn films *Uncut* and *Frankenpenis,* to show the world that he 'had recovered and was in full working order'.

Lorena in the meantime created Lorena's Red Wagon, a platform for preventing domestic violence, and has since found love with a new husband and now has a young daughter.

Her advice to the women she speaks to at her clinic for battered wives?

Never take the law into your own hands, or indeed an offending body part.

LET US
NOW PRAISE
FAMOUS ANIMALS.

THE WONDERFUL BOOK *LET US NOW PRAISE Famous Men* was published in 1941 by James Agee collaborating with photographer Walker Evans.

It poignantly illustrated the lives of sharecropper families mired in desperate poverty, and their meagre existence in America's 'Dust Bowl' prairies.

I think the time is now right for a book entitled *Let Us Now Praise Famous Animals*, if you are looking to write a sure-fire bestseller celebrating four-legged adventurers. Or, as you will read below, a one-legged one.

Pictured overleaf in 2004 is Shrek, a Merino castrated male sheep. Shrek had rebelliously run away from his flock in Tarras, New Zealand and staked out as a recluse for 6 years, living in caves in the mountains.

He survived winters on the barest sustenance, but somehow thrived.

When he was found his fleece had reached a remarkable bulk; it took 20 minutes to shear using heavy gauge electric clippers, the wool weighing in at 27kg.

The average Merino has an annual fleece weight of 4.5kg, but Shrek's coat was more than ample to produce 20 men's suits.

In a country where sheep outnumber people 10-1, Shrek

DEAD

became a national hero when his fleece was auctioned for children's medical charities, raising 150,000 NZ dollars.

He was later shorn again, to celebrate his tenth birthday, afloat an iceberg off the coast of Dunedin, New Zealand, and remained a popular national celebrity for years to come.

Sergeant Stubby was a stray, pit-bull mongrel puppy when he was taken in by an army Private, training for combat in 1917.

Named for his short tail, Stubby became the mascot of the 102nd Infantry, and took part in all activities: learning drills, bugle calls, and a modified doggy salute, bringing his paw up to his brow when he saw his new owner's fellow recruits doing it.

He was secretly smuggled aboard the SS *Minnesota* setting sail for France. Dogs were strictly forbidden on the boat, and when he was faced with an angry Commanding Officer threatening to boot him off board, he charmed him with a salute and was allowed to stay.

When they arrived in France he was even permitted to accompany the troops to the front line after they landed in 1918.

He quickly became unfazed by roaring artillery and deafening rifles, rushing up and down the trenches boosting morale.

After he was injured from a mustard gas attack, he became highly sensitive to the aroma, and this helped save the lives of his comrades on several occasions.

The assaults often took place in the early morning when everyone was sleeping, and Stubby made sure to bark and nip his comrades at the first faint whiff, to wake them up and sound the alarm.

He also had a knack for locating injured soldiers after battles, by listening out for English voices, and bringing aid to them.

One night when Stubby came across a German soldier silently mapping out the Allied trenches, he bit his ankles to trip him and kept him trapped until help came.

Stubby was promoted to Sergeant for capturing an enemy spy, the first time any non-human had received an official rank.

After 18 months and 17 battles, Stubby arrived back home to find himself on the covers of newspapers all over America.

He was awarded at least 11 medals, and met three American Presidents at the White House – Harding, Wilson, and Coolidge.

After his death in 1926, Stubby was taxidermied and is now on permanent display at the Smithsonian Museum's 'The Price of Freedom' exhibit.

One of Stubby's neighbours in the Smithsonian honour gallery is Cher Ami, a homing pigeon who also served in WWI.

Pigeons have long been enlisted in combat, and the U.S. Army used 200,000 homing pigeons over the course of WWI and WWII.

Cher Ami was an outstanding cadet who saved the lives

DEAD

of 194 survivors of the 'Lost Battalion' after the battle of Argonne Forest, France in October 1918.

554 soldiers were isolated beyond the Allied lines after the battle; many were men who had grown up on the roughest streets of New York, used to toughing it out in dangerous situations.

They found themselves without rations, and the only water supply was a stream they had to crawl to, directly beneath falling bombs.

The Germans found them easy targets, and the Battalion were constantly fighting off attacks for 6 days. Carrier pigeons were the only way for them to communicate with headquarters.

The first message they sent provided the wrong coordinates, and soon, besides enemy bombardment, they now had to contend with heavy friendly fire.

They turned to their three remaining pigeons frantically hoping to correct the mistake.

The first pigeon carried the message "Many wounded. We cannot evacuate", but was shot down.

The second carried the message "Men are suffering. Can support be sent?" He too was shot down.

Their last hope, Cher Ami, carried the message: "We are along the road Parallel 276.4. Our own troops are dropping a barrage directly on us. For heaven's sake stop it."

After delivering her missive, Cher Ami took off and immediately attracted the attention of German infantrymen who attempted to shoot her down.

She bravely flew through, dodging the pelting bullets until she was finally hit.

Managing to take flight again and return home, she arrived covered in blood; she had been shot through the breast, was blind in one eye, and one of her legs was hanging on with a single tendon.

DEAD   167

Army medics managed to save her life, but not her leg, and constructed a wooden one for her.

She delivered 12 important messages during her time at war, and like Stubby was awarded many medals

On her death she was inducted into the Racing Pigeon Hall of Fame.

Cher Ami was one of the few females on the front line; believed all her life to be a cock, it was only discovered that she was a hen after she had perished in 1919.

But she still bears the masculine version of her name, rather than the more precise Chère Amie.

DEAD

HOW TO SURVIVE BEING STABBED TO DEATH.

JULIA POPOVA WAS STABBED TO DEATH BY A mugger who plunged a seven-inch blade deep below her neck.

However, Ms Popova didn't actually die; remarkably, as you can see in the photograph here, the 22-year-old didn't feel the knife, and calmly strolled home after being left for dead, handbag stolen.

She walked into her parents' home in Moscow, in such a state of shock at the attack that she was unaware of her predicament until her horrified parents rushed her to hospital.

Surgeons managed to remove the blade without damaging Julia's spinal cord, and she made a full recovery.

Her body had released so much adrenaline in her terror, it prevented her from feeling any pain.

The remarkable powers of adrenaline have been witnessed throughout history.

Empress Elizabeth of Austria was an eccentric woman, prone to wearing very tight-laced corsets, and bouts of fasting.

She suffered from deep depressions, and an adherence to the cult of beauty that included coating her hair in treatments made of egg and cognac; her extremely long hair was prepared for 2 hours each day.

In 1898, then in her sixties, she made a visit to Geneva

incognito, despite warnings that doing so could place her in grave danger from enemies.

While out walking she was attacked by a young anarchist who seemed to stumble against her.

She fell to the ground, but later walked nearly 100 metres onto the boat that was to take her onwards on her trip.

Having boarded she collapsed once more, and on cutting open her corset a tiny brown mark was discovered on her chest – the puncture wound of the thin 6 inch long file her assassin had selected for the job.

It had pierced both her heart and a lung, making her walk back to the boat a seemingly impossible feat.

Adrenaline also provided the fuel to keep a mortally wounded Lewis Travernier alive, who at the age of 17 was shot in the face with a crossbow at the house of his friend.

Placed flat on a nearby surface the crossbow suddenly released its arrow.

In Travernier's words; "I remember hearing a snapping noise and feeling a sudden sharp pain in my cheek as my head jerked around".

In a somewhat British reaction he stoically explained that he was more mortified by the incident than anything else.

Faced by his startled friends and family in the next room he said "I felt nothing but an overriding sense of embarrassment".

Severe stabbings that prove to be non-fatal are now quite common, but there are some extreme examples.

A soldier survived being knifed four-inches directly into his forehead, the knife left lodged in his skull.

He was assumed dead by all observers. A medical team were thankfully nearby, and managed to bring the fortunate soldier back to the living, using virtuoso surgery, logistics, and team work.

It also appears that if you are to be stabbed, the best protec-

DEAD

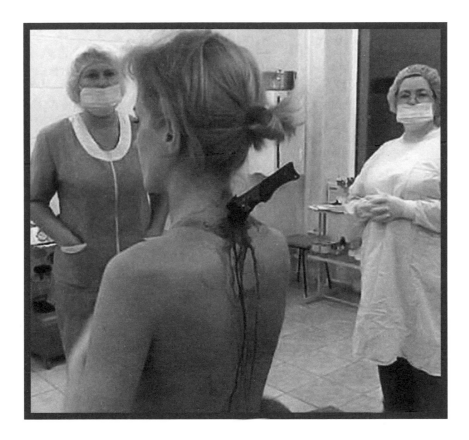

tion for you is a hearty covering of body fat.

Danny Ross was attacked in 2012, while at home in Exeter. His neighbour had come to the door to accuse him of stealing money from a family member.

Flying into a violent rage the neighbour looped his belt around Ross's neck, half-throttling him before stabbing him 38 times with a kitchen knife.

Hospital staff tactfully informed Ross that his obese frame had protected his vital organs.

Unrepentant, his attacker later tried to claim in court that Ross had deliberately stabbed himself in order to claim disability benefits.

DEAD

Stabbings are surprisingly survivable, should the victim be taken to hospital quickly.

Even after being knifed directly in the heart, 1 in 3 victims recover.

Samuel Beckett, the avant-garde novelist, playwright and theatre director, very nearly lost his life to a knife in Paris in 1938.

He was repeatedly stabbed deep in the chest having refused the solicitations of a pimp called Prudent.

James Joyce arranged for his healthcare and paid for a private room at a hospital, where Beckett finally recovered.

In the later criminal trial Beckett asked Prudent why he had stabbed him, to which the pimp replied, "I do not know sir, I'm sorry."

Danger would continue to be a facet of Beckett's young life as part of the French Resistance in 1940s occupied France. He worked as a courier, narrowly escaping capture by the Gestapo a number of times.

George Harrison, guitarist for the Beatles, was savagely stabbed by an intruder in his home.

Michael Abram, the assailant, was convinced he had been sent on a mission from God, and that Harrison's spirit had possessed him.

The Beatle and his wife fought the attacker bravely, and in court Harrison stated that when he heard his lung deflate as the knife penetrated, he truly believed that he was dying.

The police arrived in time to save the couple; Abram was diagnosed as suffering from paranoid schizophrenia.

Of course the great majority of victims do not survive serious knife assaults; one whose early departure sadly robbed the world of his unique contribution was Christopher Marlowe, the forerunner of Shakespeare.

His searing works dared to challenge the religious dogma of his day, and the mystery surrounding his death persists still.

Aged 29 he was stabbed in the eye, allegedly during a drunken tavern brawl.

This explanation never fully satisfied observers at the time, or historians ever since.

Given his open homosexuality, unbridled atheism, and service to Walsingham as a secret service member, the brawl hypothesis has always seemed a little thin.

WORTH DYING FOR.

WORTH DYING FOR IS A CHRISTIAN WORSHIP band based in California.

They are members of The Fearless Church and on their website it explains that "their fearless leaders followed the call of God to plant a vibrant, passionate church that would revolutionise culture and impact life".

Their slogan? "A sacred world needs a Fearless Church".

With a core team of twenty members they are ready to "impact the community of LA through sharing the radical love of Jesus Christ, in a real and relevant way".

I enjoyed learning about their music on the site: "Some bands are artistically innovative boundary breakers with an unwavering ability to cast their nets wide and attract an audience that literally spans all walks of life.

Others put their focus exclusively on unabashed praise and are so anointed they can literally usher listeners into the presence of God with a single strum of a chord. Worth Dying For certainly fits both impressive character profiles".

You will be delighted that their debut album made it to 166 in the Billboard Bestseller lists, and to 11 in the Top Christian Album charts.

They have stiff competition from other Christian Rock bands in California, including Born Blind, The Crucified, Die Happy, Holy Soldier, Neon Cross, Sever Your Ties, and Adam Again.

DEAD

Please don't confuse Worth Dying For with a Canadian heavy death metal band in Quebec, sharing the same name.

I doubt they share the same fan base however, so it would be confusing for their followers to attend the wrong band's gig.

Of course many millions of souls have perished in the name of religious fervour over the centuries.

But surprisingly many have died simply based on musical disputes. The 'My Way' Killings have been an ongoing phenomenon in the Philippines, where karaoke bars are wildly popular.

There have been six murders in recent years as customers have sung their version of Frank Sinatra's 1969 worldwide hit.

In May 2007 halfway through his rendition of the song, Mateo Rizal, the unfortunate singer, was shot dead by the bar's security guard.

The guard later explained that he had alerted the singer that his performance was offensively off-key, but when the young man continued to sing, the bouncer pulled out a .38 calibre pistol and shot him dead.

'Karaoke rage' is commonplace in the Philippines, where the bars have become a widespread pastime, and violence often spills out amongst the inebriated clientele.

Fights are often sparked by poor singing, or if the song performed is deemed boring.

The triumphalism of 'My Way' is, apparently, viewed as arrogant, and is best avoided from your repertoire if you are ever perfecting your vocal talents in a Manila bar.

They also, of course, take their singing prowess quite seriously in Wales.

A teenager stabbed a 45-year-old man to death because he didn't like the way he was performing a Lionel Ritchie song, 'Hello'.

He considered the singing so very poor he stabbed his victim 18 times, and slashed him repeatedly across his face, nearly succeeding in slicing off an ear.

The roll-call of killings that have resulted from playing music too loudly is a lengthy one, and spans all continents.

Young Jordan Davis was shot to death in a car for playing the radio at too high a volume.

His killer had driven up at a gas station in Atlanta alongside the car occupied by the 17-year-old Davis and three high school friends.

He asked them to turn the music down, was enraged at being ignored, and promptly fired his gun into the car.

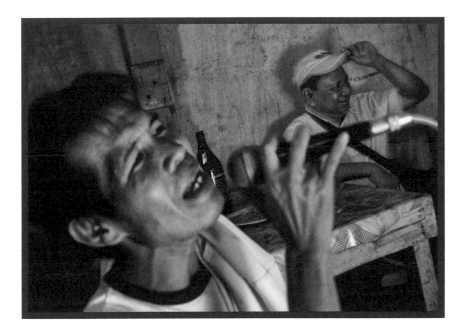

In Colorado in 2009, U.S. Special Forces soldier Richard Lopez died from head injuries he sustained in a bar brawl.

He had selected a series of songs by country rock star Jimmy Buffet on the jukebox.

Some locals took great displeasure at the selection, and a violent fight ensued, with Lopez dying later in hospital.

A resourceful couple in Sweden are my personal favourites drawn from the endless list of disputes about noisy music.

The pair, aged 71 and 81, erected a powerful sound system, with an impressively large amplifier and speaker, on their balcony.

They blasted Iron Maiden until 4am each night at their music loving neighbours, who had been disturbing their sleep for months.

The initiative did its work, and the neighbourhood's music sound levels quickly became more pleasingly harmonised.

DEAD   177

DEATH·BEFORE DISHONOUR? NOT·FOR·ME, THANKS.

LONG BEFORE 'DEATH BEFORE DISHONOUR' became the code of chivalry for Bushido, the Samurai life in Japan, it was the battle cry for the Legions led by Julius Caesar as they conquered for the Roman Empire – *Potius Mori Quam Foedari*.

Today you will find 'Death before Dishonor' tattooed across the backs of members of the U.S. Marine Corps, and engraved on a sceptre in Napoleon Bonaparte's tomb.

Outstanding people would rather die with dignity than live with dishonour and shame. But many only gain honour after they're dead.

Nathan Hale was an officer for the Continental Army during the American Revolutionary War.

During the Battle of Long Island he became a spy but was caught by British intelligence.

His famous last words, "I only regret that I have but one life to give my country," left him immortalised as an American hero.

He was hanged on 22 September 1776 but his nobility and bravery outlived him; in 1985 he was designated the state hero of Connecticut.

Of course millions have died defending their country,

but others have died because they turned their backs on their country.

Edward Donald Slovik was a private in the United States Army during WWII and was the only American soldier to be executed for desertion since the American Civil War.

Over twenty-one thousand soldiers were convicted for absconding their post during the War, which included forty nine death sentences.

But Slovik's was the only death penalty that was actually carried out.

A witness was presented who confirmed Slovik's desire to "run away". Slovik decided not to testify and the nine officers of the court found him guilty and sentenced him to be put to death.

He later wrote to General Eisenhower asking for clemency, but desertion had become a national concern, and unforgivingly Eisenhower rejected his appeal.

Slovik was 24 years old and sent to the front line for the last time, where his execution by firing squad was carried out on 31 January 1945.

It isn't merely honourable people who honour their dead.

Horst Ludwig Wessel was a leading German Nazi activist; following his violent murder in 1930 he became a posthumous hero.

The songwriter Wessel wrote the lyrics to the song 'Die Fahne Hoch' ('Raise High the Flag'), which became the Nazi Party anthem and Germany's official co-national anthem from 1933 to 1945.

The song was banned after WWII, along with all other Nazi symbols.

In Germany it still remains illegal to listen to the tune or repeat the lyrics of the Horst Wessel song.

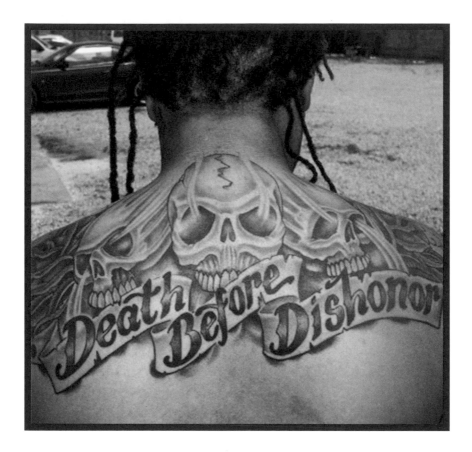

In recent years the saying, 'Death Before Dishonour' has been re-appropriated by gangs, with similar fight-or-flight mentalities to the Marine Corps.

In 2007, three members of a motorcycle outfit, also known as the 'Death Before Dishonour' gang, admitted to hunting a member of the Bandidos motorcycle club, taking him captive at Bellarine Village, and torturing him.

The gang members were reported to have committed the attack to 'prove their worth'.

In 2011 the national gang intelligence center of the Federal Bureau of Investigation stated that "There are approximately

DEAD

1.4 million active street, prison, and outlaw gang members comprising more than 33,500 gangs in the United States."

Approximately 230,000 of those gang members were in U.S. prisons.

Throughout history there have been many great men and women who died for their beliefs, to defend their country and for the greater good of humanity.

But there have also been a handful of people who have lost their lives for particularly silly causes.

Garry Hoy wanted to demonstrate that the glass used in windows of skyscrapers was unbreakable, and would regularly test the glass by running as hard as possible into it.

He was a 39-year-old senior partner at the major law firm Holden, Day, Wilson.

On 9 July 1993, Hoy decided to demonstrate how resilient the windows of his 24th storey office were in the Toronto-Dominion Centre in front of a group of interns.

He did this by hurtling towards the glass and slamming his body into the pane.

Tragically when Hoy risked his life for a second demonstration, the window gave way and he plunged to his death.

But Hoy's theory was in fact correct; the glass didn't break when he catapulted himself into it – but the windowpane just popped out of its frame.

CLINICALLY DEAD FOR 40 MINUTES, HE THEN SAT UP.

COLIN FIEDLER WAS 39 YEARS OLD WHEN HE collapsed from a heart attack in 2012 and was pronounced clinically dead at The Alfred Hospital in Victoria, Australia.

But after 40 minutes he was resurrected.

Doctors used a mechanical CPR machine called the Auto-Pulse, whilst a portable heart–lung machine kept blood and oxygen flowing to his vital organs.

Seven cardiac arrest patients in Australia have been treated with this technique; three people who had been pronounced dead have been revived, one of whom had been officially deceased for 60 minutes.

The cardiac support pump increases blood flow throughout the body more effectively than manual compressions.

The device reduces no-flow time (NFT) and squeezes the entire chest as opposed to single-spot CPR.

An AutoPulse machine was credited with saving the life of world champion swimmer Clare Carney after a 'fatal' cardiac arrest, and is now being adopted across the world.

Jim McClatchey, 54 from Atlanta, Georgia was discovered by his wife lying unconscious on floor in their house.

His heart kept seizing due to a virus. In an attempt to revive him doctors ended up shocking his chest with defibrillators 100 times.

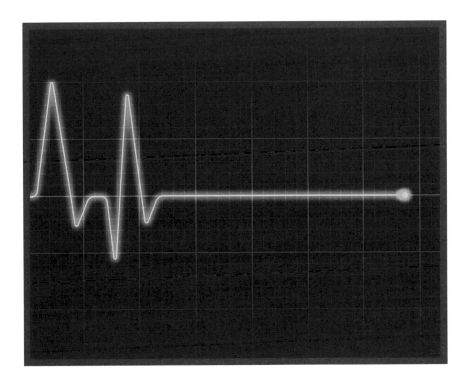

During the first hour, McClatchey's heart stopped beating for many minutes on several occasions.

The treatment was so severe he suffered second-degree burns to his chest.

But he survived, recovered and was back at work in a fortnight.

It may not be surprising that before modern day medicine and technology, there is a disturbingly long list of people who were thought dead, but in truth buried alive.

In 1896, Madame Blunden died, and she was buried after the funeral service in her family vault at Holy Ghost Chapel in Basingstoke, England.

The Blunden Vault was beneath the grounds of a school.

The day after Madam Blunden's burial, some boys heard noises coming from the vault.

DEAD

Their teacher was informed and a sexton was called. The vault and coffin were opened.

They were just moments too late to do more than watch her take her last breaths.

She had clearly been scratching the coffin frantically while trapped, wearing away all the nails from her fingers.

Due to such high numbers of premature burials between the 18th and 19th centuries a number of designs for safety coffins were developed, engineered to allow the living-corpse to signal that they've been buried alive.

Dr Timothy Clark Smith of Vermont was so worried that he may be interred while functioning that he arranged to be buried in a crypt, which featured safety precautions.

It had a connecting breathing tube and a glass window on his gravestone, which meant he could look out to the world from six feet underground.

In 1901 a woman named Madame Bobin arrived on board a steamer from Senegal.

She was pregnant and diagnosed as suffering from yellow fever.

They transferred her to a local hospital but her health began to deteriorate, and she was confirmed dead.

After Madame Bobin was buried a nurse subsequently reported that the body wasn't stone cold and that she had observed the muscles of her abdomen twitching.

She fretted that Madame Bobin could have been buried prematurely.

The father of the pregnant corpse was informed, and demanded the body be exhumed. The baby had been born and died inside the coffin, along with its mother.

An autopsy showed that she had not contracted yellow fever, but had died from asphyxiation in her tomb.

Over 1 billion people believe that Jesus rose from the dead.

According to the Bible, Jesus was crucified, resurrected and then ascended into heaven.

However, Mormons believe that he continued to live for a longer period of time and travelled from Jerusalem to America, where he taught people the new gospel.

The resurrection of Jesus has inspired a number of faiths.

Many Indian Yogis have demonstrated their ability to voluntarily slow down their heartbeat and eventually stop the organ beating for considerable periods of time.

In 1961, Dr Anand and Dr China studied three yogis who claimed they could control the pulsing of their hearts.

They reported that the yogis took a few breaths.

Then, whether they breathed normally or not, they could arrest their heartbeat for 20 seconds.

Medical experts can offer no explanation.

THE CORPSE
LEFT ON EVEREST
SINCE 1996.

THERE ARE CURRENTLY OVER 200 DEAD BODIES of fallen mountaineers on the path to Everest's peak, making it the world's highest graveyard.

Green Boots is the name given to the corpse of a victim who died on the mountain in 1996. His body is left in place and used as a marker for climbers to locate themselves on their ascent.

Poor Green Boots succumbed just a few hundred metres away from reaching the peak.

There are two reliable ways to die on Everest – traumatically and non-traumatically.

Traumatic deaths stem from bad falls, severe weather, and avalanches.

Non-traumatic fatalities are more commonplace, occurring when the climber suffers from altitude-related illness; the brain swells due to leakage of cerebral blood vessels as you reach greater heights.

Manifesting as confusion, loss of coordination and judgement, it is usually intense fatigue that is the culprit.

The climber's brain tells him he needs to sit down and rest, but the momentary pause can quickly slip into the sleep of death.

A tragic recent case was David Sharp, the British climber who sat down on his way back from the summit on 15 May 2006.

DEAD

He immediately began to freeze in place, and parties of climbers paraded past him, either believing he was already dead, or very soon to be.

Sharp was undoubtedly suffering from hypoxia – loss of oxygen – and most likely had no idea who or where he was, or felt any pain.

There are two standard routes up Everest; the north-eastern from Tibet and the south-eastern from Nepal.

All climbers who choose to start from Tibet must pass Green Boots' frozen body, where it lays just off the track.

Other bodies are scattered on the mountain – buried under rock and snow, fallen into unreachable crevasses, and sitting out in the open.

It might be startling to come to terms with the number of bodies that have been abandoned on Everest, but the reality of mountaineering is hazardous enough when attempted alone, without dragging a cumbersome extra body along with you.

However, several attempts have been made by climbers to rescue the dead and bring them to a final resting place.

Whether you are deeply religious or not, the notion of leaving someone to spend eternity face down in a crumpled heap, wearing brightly coloured climbing gear on the side of a mountain, and being stepped over by determined climbers, is not a pleasant one.

Green Boots was Indian policeman Tsewang Paljor, one of the lesser well-known victims of the 1996 Everest Disaster.

It took place on 10 and 11 May 1996, when nine people were killed in a blizzard whilst attempting to reach the summit.

The largest numbers of deaths on Everest usually occur in the aptly named 'death zone'.

It's the area of the mountain above 8,000 metres, where high elevation means oxygen is so sparse humans can't breathe unaided; that coupled with some of the most extreme weather on the planet creates a fatal concoction.

While the body can learn to tolerate such conditions, even the local Sherpa people, who have a much lower rate of death than the Westerners they guide, cannot properly acclimatise to conditions in the death zone, and are not able to breathe unaided.

It wasn't until the invention of bottled oxygen in 1922 that man attempted to reach the summit; the first attempt subsequently killed almost half of the inexperienced British expedition team.

Mankind wouldn't succeed for another 30 years when Edmund Hillary became the first to successfully ascend and descend Everest in 1953.

Since climbing duo Hillary and Tenzing Norgay, his Nepalese Sherpa, hoards of climbing hopefuls have felt driven to take up the challenge.

Sadly, there is still one death for every ten successful ascents, mostly occurring on the descent.

Hillary spoke of his outrage at how unchivalrous modern climbers have become. "I think the whole attitude towards climbing Mount Everest has become rather horrifying.

People just want to get to the top, but it is wrong if you come across a man suffering altitude problems and huddled under a rock, just to lift your hat, say good morning, and pass on by".

If you want to attempt Everest and aren't a Sherpa, I can offer two vital tips:

Eat: bulk up as much as you can before and during your trip.

On Everest your body burns 6,000 calories per day, but as you climb your appetite decreases – the body is thrown into such shock it decides that food is not necessary for survival.

Try to gain 8 kilos before you set off, as you can expect to lose 20% of your body weight during the climb.

Train: a fit body won't save you from altitude sickness, but it will help oxygen to circulate your body more efficiently.

Start training 12 months in advance – run on a treadmill for two hours each day, carrying a 15kg rucksack.

Other than altitude sickness, an array of potential ailments await you on the slopes: Alpine trench foot; coughing so hard you cough up throat tissue; cuts which won't heal at high altitudes; frostbite that turns your flesh cloudy white (still some hope) or black (hopeless), hypothermia, broken bones, sunburn (particularly common on the roof of the mouth due to the sun's reflection and panting for air), hallucinations, and thrombosis which thickens your blood to the consistency of custard.

DEAD

How much does it cost to risk death on Everest?

You'll need £30,000 for the 70 day trip as part of an expedition. This doesn't include insurance (£1,300), flights to and from Kathmandu (£900), your clothing and equipment (£4,000), and an advanced snow and ice climbing course (£650).

Money well spent, I'm sure.

EVEN·A·DEAD·CAT
WILL·BOUNCE·IF
DROPPED·FROM·A
GREAT·HEIGHT.

THIS EXPRESSION IS USED IN FINANCIAL circles to illustrate a small, brief recovery in the price of a declining stock.

Wider usage has been adopted to describe any temporary appearance of recuperation that turns out to be illusory.

Stock market jargon provides a darkly amusing insight into the vagaries of the financial world; 'gentlemen prefer bonds' was the term bandied about Wall Street, referring to the fact that bonds tend to outperform stocks during a recession.

The Misery Index was a term developed by Jimmy Carter during his Presidency in the 1970s, and describes the unemployment rate and inflation rate added together.

This rate was highest during his and his predecessor Gerald Ford's terms in government, with a score of 16.26. Barak Obama stands lower on this grim table, with a score of 10.75.

Also indicative of the rollercoaster dives that repeatedly occur in global economies is in the number of 'black' days – there has been a Black Monday, a Black Tuesday, and a Black Friday, amongst others.

The latter was sparked in 1869 by just two speculators, trying to corner the market in gold, and artificially increase its price through manipulating those close to the President, Ulysses S. Grant.

DEAD

The resultant crash would taint Grant with scandal for life.

Black Monday took place in 1987, when a collapse originated in Hong Kong and spread west to Europe like wildfire.

Eventually hitting the U.S., it wiped out almost a quarter of its stock market value in 24 hours.

They fared better, however, than New Zealand which lost 60% of its stock market worth in the global panic.

Black Tuesday, the great Wall Street Crash, shook American confidence to its core.

The most devastating panic in financial history sparked a world wide depression that lasted 10 years.

At its lowest point the Dow Jones Index of stock values lost a breath-taking 89% of its market value.

DEAD

Newspapers at the time carried stories of bankers flinging themselves from their skyscraper offices as stock price fell through the floor.

But the widespread suicide of bankers in 1929 was little more than a myth; in reality the number of suicides in New York in the month following the crash were actually lower than usual.

Eight people did jump from buildings in the city, though only two of these were on Wall Street.

What is undeniable is the strong linkage between high unemployment and suicide, the rates of which rise fiercely during recessions and times of austerity.

Interestingly the only thing that finally put paid to the Great Depression was America's mobilisation for WWII.

This perfectly encapsulated the conspiracy theory mantra about the military/industrial complex – if business needs a boost, get involved in a war.

Every speculative financial meteoric rise 'bubble' adheres to the 'greater fool' theory; you will make a questionable investment because you believe that the person you will be selling to will be a greater fool.

Of course, by their nature, like the dot-com bubble, they eventually pop; the conditions for success rely on market optimism and momentum, and that the 'greater fool' will be around to offload to, just in time for canny investors to withdraw.

The manipulation of the market to this knowing degree is now known as 'pump and dump'.

Low value company stock is misleadingly promoted as a sound quick-turn investment, prompting speculators to buy the shares more expensively.

As the price is driven up, the stock is portrayed ever more flatteringly, until the original buyers dump their shares and the price bottoms out.

The internet has made this kind of fraud much easier through the advent of spam marketing campaigns and investment message boards.

A 15-year-old, Jonathan Lebed, manipulated investors in this way during the great dot-com boom.

He bought penny stocks and promoted them on message boards, before selling out at a high price.

A suit was filed against him, which he paid off through a fraction of his gains, and 'promised not to do it again'.

In 2001 Enron won the 'pump and dump' crown, with 29 executives selling wildly over-valued stock for more than a billion dollars, just before the company went bankrupt.

Perhaps the greatest white collar criminal of all time is the previous Chairman of NASDAQ, Bernie Madoff.

In 2009 he pleaded guilty to 11 federal crimes and was sentenced to 150 years in prison for his creation of the biggest Ponzi scheme the world has seen.

In this system, investors are paid returns from the investments of those who have just bought into the package.

They are enticed by high rates of return that seem highly profitable and reliably consistent.

Madoff had 4,800 clients, and the size of his fraud is estimated at $64.8 billion.

The scheme unraveled in 2008 with the general market downturn, and Madoff had nowhere near enough cash to pay back investors who needed their money.

Suddenly, there was no 'greater fool' for Madoff to find.

THE
DEAD MAN'S
SWITCH.

IT HAS TWO APPLICATIONS: A KILL-SWITCH that automatically cuts power if the operator of a locomotive, tube train, tractor, chainsaw, personal watercraft etc is incapacitated through death or loss of consciousness.

Application two is also a kill-switch, but in a more sinister sense; it activates a bomb vest or an IED, when the holder of the weapon is clutching a switch that will explode the weapon if the hand is released e.g. if the holder is shot or killed.

This scenario assumes that the bomber is holding hostages, or is standing somewhere crowded with people – and doesn't mind dying, as long as many others die simultaneously.

Militarily, the Dead Hand system was the Cold War era nuclear-control strategy that acted as a deterrent; it guaranteed mutual annihilation by maintaining an automated second-strike capability even greater than any first strike delivered by an opponent.

A Dead Man's Switch was originally developed as a safety measure, in the event that someone operating a machine becomes incapacitated, either losing consciousness or dying.

Recently, an American top level government insider put his own Dead Man's Switch into play.

Whistleblower Edward Snowden startled the world in the summer of 2013 with his revelatory interview describing America's surveillance agencies.

Snowden is a former senior employee of NSA, the National Security Agency that is dedicated to cryptology.

It specialises in collecting and monitoring the foreign emails and phone conversations that are routed through the U.S.

As America is often the cheapest technical carrier from one external country to another, it can listen in on the majority of the world's conversations.

The prime mission of this continual collating is regarded as vitally important in combatting terrorism.

The NSA was established after the 2001 attacks in New York, hoping to snuff out potential national threats before they have a chance to develop.

But the definitions of what constitutes terrorism are far from clear cut, and surveillance is being undertaken on people who are apparently law-abiding American citizens, as well as suspicious foreigners.

By offering fees to phone operators and internet giants like Google and Facebook, the NSA are able to access the back end of the services they provide, harvesting an individual's conversations and storing them for the future.

An organisation called Prism is able to tap into various web servers and collect everything from the computer you use, your photographs, videos, internet history, bank details etc.

Risking his own safety, Snowden gave an interview with two

journalists from the *Guardian*, and a documentary filmmaker, in a hotel in Hong Kong.

His aim was to heighten awareness about the NSA's activities.

He stated that if he failed to speak out, despite the obvious personal risks, he "would be allowing the world to turn into an Orwellian nightmare for future generations; this is just the beginning of extending the capabilities of an architecture of repression".

Despite these being the biggest intelligence leaks in recent history, Snowden remained vocal and visible, while American officials were calling him a traitor "revealing this information to potential enemies, jeopardising his own country's safety".

Snowden argues that terrorists would have to be ineffectively amateur not to know that this kind of surveillance was being undertaken, and must already be working around it.

Snowden has been charged with espionage in the U.S., and moved to Russia.

Despite the U.S. asking for him to be extradited, he has been granted asylum for a year, after which time he will move on to a Southern American country, several of whom have already granted his permanent asylum.

In an tactical move, Snowden released more locked files of information to a number of organisations.

His Dead Man's Switch came into operation here; Snowden has made it clear that if he is involved in a mysterious and fatal accident, the holders of the locked files will find themselves in the possession of the decryption key to unlock the data and be free to publish it all.

President Obama, however, continues to maintain that no American people have been listened to, or had their data collected.

However, he also stated that "We don't have to sacrifice our freedom in order to achieve security, but we do need to make trade-offs."

The NSA is the largest employer of mathematicians in the world, all of whom are given endless problems to solve without knowing what their application might be.

It was intriguing to learn that Google have now developed a new feature called Inactive Account Manager, which is a Dead Man's Switch that allows people to plan their 'digital afterlife'.

Rather than your emails and digital archives dying with you, or being destroyed when you can no longer use your account, Google's Dead Man's Switch can now immortalise your cyber-archives.

You can administer all your data so that it autodestructs and is deleted after three, six, nine or twelve months of inactivity.

Or your data can be passed down and inherited by a select few chosen contacts.

Inactive Account Manager becomes an extension of a person's Will.

Another useful feature is that you can create a custom designed alarm system: "Email Amnesty International and tell them I'm in jail", or "Email my children and tell them I'm dead and give them instructions for probating my estate".

Being dead may not stop you being a menace to society.

In Britain, one worrying source of air pollution is caused by mercury in dental fillings being emitted into the atmosphere when bodies are cremated. The government has ordered crematoriums to eliminate their emissions by the end of the decade.

Casket manufacturers are one of the 50 most ecologically unsound material waste producers, thanks to the toxic resistant finishes they apply.

On a conventional 10-acre cemetery site, there is enough casket wood to build over forty houses, plus over 900 tons of

casket steel, 20,000 tons of vault concrete, and enough formalin to fill a swimming pool.

It appears that however nice you may be in life, in death you end up as expensive, hazardous waste.

DYING FOR SEX 24 HOURS A DAY.

AMERICA IS THE WORLD LEADER IN DEATHS resulting from sex.

One in every 100 deaths each year in the U.S. is sex related, not including fatalities caused by the AIDS/HIV infection.

This is three times higher than anywhere else in the world; often as the result of heart attacks during the activity, but also from sex games gone awry, involving bondage, S&M, and autoeroticism.

A 2011 analysis by the *Journal of Sexual Medicine* found that men who are unfaithful are more likely to die through fatal cardiac arrests during sex than faithful men, typically with a younger partner in an unfamiliar location.

They estimated that 90% of sex-deaths are male, with 75% of those having extra-marital sex.

Drugs like Viagra have been found to make sex more hazardous, especially in older men, or men with existing heart conditions.

Young men are also at risk, taking the drug recreationally without a prescription, and prone to overdose.

During sex you are anywhere from 2 to 7 times more likely to have a heart attack than with mere exercise, due to the increases in blood pressure and heart rate, especially during orgasm.

The majority of AIDS transmissions worldwide occur through heterosexual sexual contact, rather than by infected drug users sharing needles.

However in the U.S. and UK, AIDS/HIV is most frequently passed between homosexual men, about 60% of new sufferers each year.

The spread of the infection is most common in low income countries, and is especially rife in Africa.

Africa is home to 15% of the world's population but distressingly accounts for 70% of the world's AIDS/HIV fatalities each year.

In developed countries, deaths from other sexually transmitted diseases, like syphilis, are now far rarer than in previous eras.

Whilst sex has proven health benefits, what are the risks generally involved in sex other than for people with weak hearts?

Erotic asphyxiation is the purposeful deprivation of oxygen to the brain for sexual arousal, often through strangulation.

Somebody who enjoys this peccadillo is known as a gasper.

The sensation delivered is reportedly so intense that the brain induces a lucid, hallucinogenic state that, when combined with orgasm, creates a rush as powerful as cocaine, and even more addictive.

Surprisingly, the technique was first practised in the 17th century as a treatment for erectile dysfunction.

Doctors noticed the 'death erections' of male victims at public hangings and thought this was the cure they were seeking for impotent men.

It certainly brings a picturesque new meaning to the French term for orgasm, *la petite mort*, or 'little death'.

But even amongst hard core practitioners sex games can go wrong; Simon Burley strangled to death in 2007 whilst his girlfriend desperately tried to cut him down with a blunt knife, dressed as a neo-Nazi executioner.

It's not just men who suffer fatal accidents.

Kirsten Taylor's husband told police that his wife had been shocked by her hair dryer, when they were inquiring into her death in 2008.

He later admitted that he had been electrocuting her nipples, and that the couple had been partaking in 'electric shock sex' for two years prior without a hiccup.

But you don't have to have a penchant for S&M to die from lust.

32-year-old Japanese couple Sachi and Tomio Hidaka, remained virginal while they were together for 14 years, before they got married in 1992.

They were so shy and conservative that they decided to wait till their wedding night to consummate their relationship.

Tragically, both died of heart attacks during their first experience.

Félix Faure, who was the French President from 1895 till his death in 1899, was a moustached silver fox who was popular with society ladies.

He died of sudden apoplexy during a rendezvous with Marguerite Steinheil, a favourite mistress, whilst she was fellating him.

His hands stiffened as he grabbed violently at her hair, and poor Ms Steinheil was so alarmed that she got lockjaw, and had to be removed from his corpse by doctors using a crowbar.

The incident gave her the nickname *la pompe funèbre*, which has a double meaning in translation: 'death care business' or 'funeral fellatio'.

A more recent memorable night of passion was the legacy of Nigerian businessman and philanthropist Uroko Onoja.

He enjoyed a lifestyle that some men would consider an enviable arrangement: six wives, all desperately in love with him.

However, this appealing situation was not so idyllic in reality. The women proved that they were not as doe-eyed and subservient as Onoja would have imagined, but instead jealous and cunning.

In 2012 Onoja's marital set-up took a grisly turn when he returned from the local pub.

He headed, as usual, to the room of his youngest and pret-

tiest wife. Whilst in the throes of passion, his other five wives burst in wielding knives and clubs, demanding that he pay them some attention for a change, and have sex with all of them immediatcly.

Onoja made a hearty attempt to fulfil his husbandly duties and satisfy his harem; he made it through wives 6-2, but when the final wife approached the bed she found him totally expired.

His heart had finally given out. The other wives, seeing the last wife on the list trying to revive her dead husband, ran away into the street giggling.

Two of the wives were arrested, and the police report on the incident described his demise as "raped to death".

Clearly it was regarded as a comical, good way to go. But probably not by the late Mr Onoja.

WHEN THE GAME ENDS, THE KING AND PAWN GO IN THE SAME BOX.

NAPOLEON BELIEVED WE ARE ALL EITHER kings, or pawns.

But even if you are one of those sent to fight on the front line, rather than a nobleman or general who stands behind it, he declared that everyone will end up the same.

Kings or pawns, we are all relegated to becoming merely the bones of dead men, whether held in makeshift rickety coffins, or the most magnificent of tombs.

Just as chess players take the lives of an opponent's pieces, eventually checkmating the king, death has also taken a cruel toll among many of the greatest chess players.

On 21 June 1851, Adolf Anderson and Lionel Kieseritzky played a game in London, during the first international chess tournament.

Anderson sacrificed both of his rooks, a bishop and later his queen, beating his opponent with his three remaining minor pieces. His bold and fearless victory led to it later being named the 'Immortal Game'.

Two years later, his opponent Lionel Kieseritzky, one of the foremost grandmasters of chess, died in a charity hospital for the insane in Paris, and was buried in a pauper's grave, only to be still remembered for his startling defeat.

Chess players whose crystal logic turned to madness include former world champion William Steinitz.

In 1900 Steinitz died in Manhattan State Hospital, hospitalised, diagnosed and confined as insane, after being committed there by his wife.

Henry Pilsbury, another master, was institutionalised in an asylum in Pennsylvania, where he died in 1906.

His obituary in the *New York Times*, stated that he died from an "illness contracted through over-exertion of his brain cells".

Even compilers of chess problems can finally end their days maddened by the game; William Russ committed suicide at the age of thirty-three, in 1866. He had adopted an eleven-year-old girl and when she was twenty-one he proposed to her. She refused to marry him, so he shot her four times in the head; remarkably she survived.

Russ then attempted suicide by drowning himself in the local river, but failed, so he fired a bullet into his brain and finally died ten days later in hospital.

In 1959 two scientists were playing a chess match in a Soviet research station in Vostok, Antarctica.

At the end of the game, they got into a fierce argument and the losing player was so frustrated and enraged he buried an axe into his comrade's skull. Chess was promptly banned in Antartic stations.

Born in 1974, Alexander Pichushkin is a Russian serial murderer.

Known as 'The Chessboard Killer' he is thought to have killed up to 63 people in southwest Moscow's Bitsa Park, where several of his victim's bodies were found.

In his early childhood, Pichushkin is remembered to have been a very sociable child. However, after being hit on the head by a metal swing, he became exceptionally hostile and aggressive and was transferred to a school for children with learning disabilities.

The humiliating degradation of being labelled a backward child led him to be excluded and bullied by other youngsters.

In the early stages of his adolescence, Pichushkin's grandfather saw that he was highly intelligent.

He decided to have Pichushkin live with him and encouraged extra-curricular activities. He was taught how to play chess and taken regularly to watch the public games played in Bitsa Park.

He became an exceptional player and dominated the chessboard.

However, he continued to be tormented by other schoolchildren and during his late teens his grandfather died, leaving him bereft and lonely.

Pichushkin began to drink vodka heavily, but it did not affect his ability to play advanced chess. His slide into becoming a psychopath started when he began to carry a little video camera everywhere, and would record himself threatening young children.

Alexander would enjoy watching these later, played back for himself many times. Pichushkin stated that he had aimed to kill 64 people, the number of squares on a chessboard.

He mainly targeted elderly homeless men, and after drinking vodka with them Pichushkin would knock them senseless with a hammer.

He would then stab the vodka bottles into their heads, to be certain there were no survivors.

Tragically, he also enjoyed killing many children and women.

He was convicted in 2007 for 49 murders, and three attempted murders. He asked for an additional 11 victims to be added to his tally and was sentenced to a life term, after he was declared legally sane.

The first 15 years of his imprisonment were ordered to be spent in solitary confinement.

Rather echoing Bonaparte's view that we are all equal after death, history is littered with countless, nameless corpses that have been with treated with little respect, stacked in the ground like cattle in a slaughterhouse.

In Peru in 2012, a tomb was discovered at the temple of Pachacamac, where twenty pyramids were found; buried inside were dozens of human skeletons. The remains of bodies were placed methodically to create patterns, interpreted as evidence of many human sacrifices.

A closer examination revealed that the adult skeletons were arranged inside a circle of baby skeletons. Within the temple, the sacrifices were carried out by the Ychsma, an ancient people who pre-dated the Incas.

It appears that the babies' bodies found inside the ring of the dead belonged to pilgrims, who had traveled to meet the Ychsma tribe in search of spiritual guidance, and paid a terrible price for their innocence.

On Hart Island, which was used as a prisoner of war camp during the U.S. Civil War in 1865, many hundreds of bodies of Confederate and Union soldiers were buried together in a vast single pit.

The remains of Union soldiers, identified by their uniforms, were eventually excavated and relocated.

The killing fields in Cambodia offer an insight into the genocides carried out under one of the most venomous dictators of all time, Pol Pot.

After the Cambodian Civil War of 1975–9, 20,000 mass gravesites were found built in his name, containing over 1.38 million bodies.

The killed were those suspected of being allied to the former government; intellectuals, professionals and a wide variety of ethnic and religious groups, whom his regime decided to eradicate.

Also horrifying was the 'Maguindanao Massacre' which took place only four years ago.

An election was underway in Maguindanao, in the Philippines. Two rival members of one political party were running for the same office.

Vice-Mayor Esmael 'Toto' Mangudadatu was going to file for his certificate of candidacy, but received threats that his rival would kill him, in an unpleasant and protracted way, if he persisted.

He decided to protect himself by inviting thirty-seven journalists to accompany him.

One hundred heavily armed men stopped his caravan, and Mangudadtu's entire entourage were slaughtered. 58 were killed, with some female journalists brutally gang-raped and then shot in the genitals.

A vast grave had been dug two days before the massacre, in preparation, large enough to bury the dead with their vehicles.

Too late to do more than watch and film the atrocity, hovering high above was a helicopter, which helped to track and capture the killers.

And to bring justice down upon the political rival, who was prepared to win his office at any price.

YOU·REALLY CAN·DIE·OF EMBARRASSMENT.

A REPORT PUBLISHED IN THE BRITISH Medical Journal in 1860 described a case where a housemaid was caught red-handed stealing food from a larder.

Upon being discovered, she dropped dead on the spot.

Doctors at the time were unable to diagnose her demise, but now we know it was a sudden rush of adrenaline – the residue of a particularly humiliating experience which produced heightened anxiety and stress.

More recently in 2008, Juncnok Park a former Buddhist monk and then Oxford student, committed suicide just hours after being told his PhD thesis needed to be improved.

He had served ten years under holy orders in South Korea and after receiving a scholarship to read Oriental Studies in 2003 he devoted himself to gaining a doctorate in Buddhism.

Examiners believed he was not yet ready to be awarded a doctorate. Park considered this so gravely shaming, he hung himself.

Sowon Park was a friend of the graduate and noted that "This must have been a real shock to him, as he had never failed anything in his life".

In 2012, at the age of 15 Audrie Pott committed suicide eight days after three boys had sexually assaulted her; photos of the abuse had been circulated online.

She had attended a friend's house party in Northern California, but after getting intoxicated she passed out.

When she woke, she realised that she had been sexually assaulted; her attackers had drawn on intimate parts of her body in magic marker, whilst she was unconscious.

She had known the accused boys since Junior High.

The next day in school, a group of students were huddled around a mobile phone and she learnt that humiliating photos of her exposed and abused were being circulated.

She posted a message to a friend via Facebook that said, "I have a reputation for a night I don't even remember, and the whole school knows".

As a victim of sexual abuse, alongside the social humiliation, she found it impossible to cope and took her own life.

Each of the boys involved was charged with sexual battery, and dissemination of child pornography, under California law at the time.

Bizarrely, these less severe charges are filed if a victim is unconscious and does not have the ability to fight off a sexual assault.

As a result of this horrible case, and others similar, laws are finally being reviewed.

Amongst those who die from embarrassment less directly are the poor souls who postpone, or fail to report a serious medical condition because of its nature. By the time they do, it is often too late.

Men who are reluctant to seek medical advice or treatment for prostate cancer are truly dying of embarrassment.

Approximately 19,500 men in the UK are diagnosed with the disease each year. Of these, 9,500 will die.

Doctors report that men who ignore the early symptoms of the disease, because they're too self-conscious to seek help, increase the risk of dying significantly.

They predict that over the next decade prostate cancer will become the most commonly diagnosed form of the disease, above lung and breast cancer.

Surprisingly, even though we may not think of men suffering from breast cancer, over 400 men lose their lives in this way each year.

This is largely due to waiting longer to seek medical treatment, and the gender confusion of the term.

Men do not think that they could possibly have breast cancer, because they do not posses functional breasts.

A report published by Johns Hopkins University also revealed that many young people in the United States are dying prematurely of AIDS for similar reasons.

Hopefully, you have never been so humiliated that you wanted to kill yourself; nonetheless you could still suffer an embarrassing death.

In 1986, a woman was found in Dayton, Ohio, naked and trapped underneath her lover's corpse.

The couple had parked their car on an upper storey of a little-used public garage, but whilst they were having sex in the back seat of the car, he suddenly dropped dead.

He collapsed on top of her, and his heavy body pinned her to the back seat.

Unable to move, by the time she was discovered his body had begun to decompose on top of her.

She was dehydrated and suffering from hypothermia. Within a couple of hours of being rescued, she also died.

Obesity has become became a modern plague in the West, in a society where people are left salivating at every delightful food commercial on TV.

Ironically, in the richest nations, the poorest citizens have become the fattest.

To be very overweight was once a symbol of wealth in many ancient cultures.

In the 1950s being a super-plus size made Robert Earl Hughes a minor celebrity, weighing in at a magnificent 486kg.

However, he died at the age of 32 as a result of his overwhelming girth.

His death was not as graceful or dignified as his fans may have hoped.

He was much too heavy to be carried out by a strong crew of men, and he had to be hoisted from his deathbed by a crane.

He was later buried in a coffin made from a reconstructed grand piano crate.

Sexual perversion causes many less-than-glorious deaths, like that of 53-year-old photographer Dieter Lorz.

He was discovered dead in his Stuttgart apartment in 1985 with homemade electrodes attached to his testicles and a rubber ball-gag in his mouth.

His death was described as "an embarrassing, unusual, but self-inflicted accident".

More prosaically, the Experian survey carried out at King's College London revealed that people are no longer willing to live with old-fashioned English surnames such as Smellie, Bottom, Balls, and Cock.

When these ancient names were first applied in Medieval times it was unlikely that they were thought of as rude or lewd.

The surname Balls was not an indication of sexual prowess or courage.

Rather, it was legendarily inherited if your father had the admirable first name Balle, greatly respected amongst Vikings.

GET TO HEAVEN AN HOUR BEFORE THE DEVIL KNOWS YOU'RE DEAD.

THE ORIGINS FOR THIS STRANGELY PRECISE instruction stem from particular blend of Irish folklore and Christian mythology.

The phrase is commonly used as a blessing at weddings or funerals. "May your glass be ever full. May the roof over your head be always strong. And may you be in heaven an hour before the devil knows you're dead."

The meaning of the saying seems to point to the belief that during the time between death and burial, the body of the deceased must be closely guarded; this is the dangerous moment in which the devil could steal away your soul.

Traditional Irish funerals focus on your existence immediately after your death.

Often the body will lie at home, and friends and relatives will come to pay their respects, drink tea or whiskey, and reminisce.

The corpse will usually be laid out in white linen and be displayed on their bed, never to be left alone, protecting it from the Devil.

The wake would last from the time of death until the actual funeral service, and would necessitate a series of ritualistic observances out of respect for the departed.

All the clocks in the house would be stopped, all mirrors

turned around, the body bathed and dressed. A deceased man's face would be shaved, a woman's made up.

When the body is prepared, the women of the house would begin a plaintive cry or wail known as keening.

This is undertaken to both display grief and to ward off evil spirits who would surround the body.

Irish folklore to mark a death is probably more renowned for the accompanying drinking, dancing and hearty partying, that gives the deceased a rousing send off.

The Catholic Church tried numerous times throughout Irish history to ban the drinking of alcohol during wakes, but unsurprisingly failed in their efforts.

In some parts of Ireland it is traditional to play a game of cards and deal one hand for the departed.

Although the practice of carrying out these post-death activities is waning in Ireland in favour of funeral parlours, the wake is still an integral part of the ceremonies around death in rural areas.

Reaching further back into Irish mythology, the death of a loved one is usually heralded by a Banshee, or Bean Sí.

This woman of the fairy mounds is a messenger from the Otherworld, and her wail signals an imminent death.

She is often depicted washing the bloodstained clothes or armour of someone who has died and she can be portrayed as ravishingly beautiful, or an exceptionally grotesque old hag.

Apparently, it is usually unfortunate to see a Banshee on your travels; to meet one in person suggests that you are to die a violent death.

King James I of Scotland was approached by a Banshee before his murder in a sewer of his castle, where he had fled when trying to escape his murderers.

The Banshee call is described differently throughout Ireland.

In Tyrone it is 'the sound of two boards being struck together', whilst in Kerry it is a low pleasant singing. The Banshees have sisters known as the Banach, who haunt battlefields.

In Celtic mythology the Otherworld was a realm of the dead and the home of spirits and gods.

Part of druidic lore, the Otherworld was believed to lie alongside the living world, or to be located on certain islands, such as Anglesey on the Welsh coast, a sacred spot for British druids.

In Irish myth the Otherworld is often described as a paradise, filled with endless happiness.

It is always summer, with no sickness or old age, bearing a striking resemblance to the Ancient Greek/Roman Elysium.

The Otherworld was co-opted by the Christian faith, which aimed to try and draw parallels between pagan and Catholic belief, to make it more palatable to the cultures where missionaries were spreading their system of religion.

Scholars have since argued that the Otherworld was actually a many-layered realm, comprising of different worlds such as Tech Duinn, a place for the dead made up of good and evil.

Various gods lived here including Donn, an aloof figure that Christianity took up as the Devil, and the cause of shipwrecks and storms.

The gates to the Otherworld would open once a year, on 31 October, when souls who had been betrayed in our world were freed to walk amongst the living, and exact their revenge.

Called Samhaim, this was to become Halloween.

The Banshees must have been wailing to deafening levels in 1988, when Michael Stone, a Ulster Defence Association volunteer attacked an IRA funeral single-handedly, with grenades and pistols.

Almost lynched by the furious crowd, he was rescued by police and has been held in prison ever since.

His assault killed three people and wounded more than 60 in an event that was horrifying not only for its brutality, but for its irreverent and cynical targeting of a mourning crowd at a graveyard.

High ranking members of the IRA were present, and the slaughter piled further controversy on the killings of the three IRA members whose funerals were being held.

Daniel McCann, Sean Savage and Mairead Farrell had been shot dead by the SAS in Gibraltar, apparently whilst unarmed and without warning.

Their assassination had caused widespread outrage, but Michael Stone, when interrogated by police, claimed that his act was in vengeance for the Remembrance Day bombings by the IRA four months earlier.

The British Cenotaph had been attacked, with eleven people killed and 63 injured – an event that even diehard IRA members had been dismayed by; they suspected that its unwarranted viciousness had irredeemably hampered the Republican cause.

In any event, the Banshee, the Bannach and Donn must have looked down with much satisfaction, and wholehearted wailing.

ARE YOV BEING BORED TO DEATH BY THIS BOOK?

SCIENTISTS HAVE DECIDED THAT BOREDOM shaves years of your life.

They decree that "High levels of tedium make you twice as likely to die from heart disease or a stroke than people who are content and fulfilled."

Over a period of 25 years their report observed over 7,000 civil servants and found that those who said they suffered from boredom were almost 40 percent more likely to die by the end of the study than those who didn't. Women were more than 20 times likely to suffer from boredom than men.

In *The Plague* Albert Camus wrote that the truth is that everyone is bored, and devote themselves to cultivating habits.

It certainly makes for boring reading to be endlessly warned that you can clinically increase your premature death by cigarette smoking, excessive eating, lack of exercise, and large quantities of alcohol.

I like them all equally, and would certainly die prematurely of boredom without them.

A large scale study interviewed and observed the lifestyle habits of about 80,000 female nurses, beginning in 1980. At the start of the study, none of the women suffered from pre-existing medical conditions of note.

During the 24 year period, there were 8,882 deaths.

1,790 died from cardiovascular disease, and a further 4,527 from cancer.

DEAD   217

Depressingly, 55% of those deaths had demonstrable correlations to smoking, low physical activity, being overweight and alcohol intake.

But if you're currently reading this whilst drinking a glass of wine, do not fear.

The nurses with a light to moderate alcohol intake, up to one drink daily, were less likely to die from cardiovascular disease than those who didn't drink any alcohol.

Sadly, whilst reading this book your sedentary behaviour could increase lethargy and depression levels.

A good doctor would urge you to put this book down, and have sex; scientists agree that frequent mating can actually improve health, and double life expectancy.

Over the course of a decade a study at Queens University in Belfast that was published in the *British Medical Journal*, recording the sexual activities of about 1,000 middle-aged men.

It compared men of a similar age and health and discovered that men who reported the highest frequency of orgasm lived twice as long as those who did not enjoy sex.

Sex has been proven to lower blood pressure, improve cholesterol, and increase circulation.

During sex the heartbeat increases from 70 to 150 beats per minute. People who enjoy lovemaking regularly are half as likely to suffer from heart attacks and strokes than those who don't have sex at all.

An active sex life can also increase weight loss – 30 minutes will burn 200 calories. It also stimulates the production of phenethylamine, which is a natural amphetamine that regulates the appetite and reduces food cravings.

Having regular orgasms can act as a preventative measure against coughs and colds. Sex releases an antibody called immunoglobulin A, which boosts immunity and at the moment of climax a chemical called DHEA is released, which also balances the immune system.

Masturbating regularly is absolutely acceptable medically. But not to maniacal levels.

A young man aged 16 was found dead after masturbating continuously 42 times during one night in Brazil. His mother told local newspapers that she was aware of her son's addiction, but it was too late before she could seek help. His computer contained a bewildering amount of pornography, with approximately 17 million erotic videos and 600 million explicit photographs.

The *Telegraph* reported that a retired Church minister advised that terminally ill people should distract themselves from thoughts of dying by reading 'saucy' books.

The pamphlet, written by the Reverend Ian Gregory, prepares people for death and advises people not to read The Bible.

Instead he suggests that people should read "a romance book or a bodice ripper", to make their last moments a little more pleasurable.

The founder of the UKs Polite Society and Campaign for Courtesy supported the Reverend's liberal views by saying that, "The subject of death is still a bit taboo, like sex used to be, so why not? It might trigger some happy, joyful, rude memories".

It is far harder to be bored in today's modern world than it used to be in the past.

In a single day we process more information than somebody living in the 15th century would manage in an entire lifetime.

Perhaps it is still the case that the cure for boredom remains simply a curiosity to learn.

Research again shows that life expectancy is, even today, an issue of class – with socioeconomic factors determining life expectancy.

People with lower incomes and lower education levels have higher death rates after heart attacks.

In 2008, researchers from the Mayo Clinic presented new data which illustrated that affluent people were more likely to survive a heart attack than people with lower income, literacy levels, and education.

They examined medical records from 705 patients who were treated after a heart seizure.

Researchers recorded the years of schooling completed, and contrasting income levels. 85% of people who survived were those with more than 12 years of education. Those from less favoured backgrounds achieved a survival rate in the low 60s.

Cardiovascular researcher Dr Gerber stated that, "education is strongly associated with health literacy, which in turn affects one's ability to obtain, process, and understand basic health information and services needed to make appropriate health decisions."

According to today's Gospel, The *Daily Mail*, boredom is one of the world's top killers. It creates a vacuum that leads to harmful habits like smoking and drinking, out of lethargy.

If you are in a dull job, their invaluable advice is to "find outside interests".

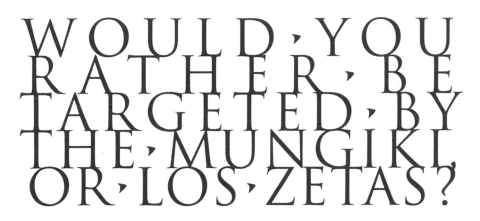

WOULD·YOU RATHER·BE TARGETED·BY THE·MUNGIKI, OR·LOS·ZETAS?

STREET GANGS CAN GROW FROM A TROUBLEsome clan of local young hooligans into something like the Bloods, or the Crips.

These are two rival outfits, 30,000 members strong each, that have been duelling for territorial control on the streets of Los Angeles since 1970.

Sadly, neither is considered worthy of nomination to the Hall of Fame of the most fearsome, most powerful, and richest criminal organisations the world now has to offer.

None of them has the allure, or the warm familial bonds of the Mafia, with charismatic Sicilian Dons heading up each congenial branch.

Today's leading gangs don't follow the paternal advice of the Godfather, "Keep your friends close and your enemies closer".

The Mara Salvatrucha make no distinction between friends and enemies, and have little hesitation in killing anyone for any reason.

MS13 as it is more cosily known, was formed in the 1980s with a mix of Guatemalans, Hondurans, Salvadorans, and Central Americans.

Today it is considered the world's most terrifying crime gang, and operations have spread into the U.S., Spain, Britain, Germany, and Canada.

DEAD   221

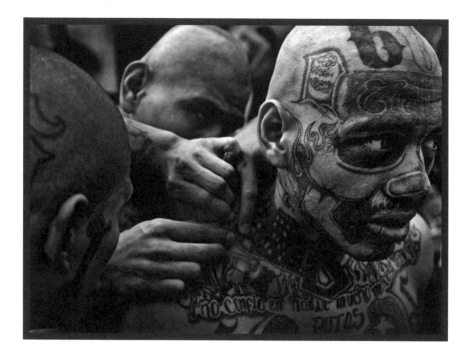

They have no time for remorse, and have no qualms about killing civilians; they firebombed a bus full of women and children, killing all 28 passengers.

The Mungiki is centered around Nairobi in Kenya, and is made up of cells across Africa.

They don't like Christianity or any attempt to Westernise the continent, and show their displeasure by beheadings, mutilations involving limb removal, and female genital cutting.

They murder police officers as a matter of routine, and have grown wealthy enough to draw on their own paramilitary forces whenever threatened, even by governments.

Unlike most gangs who identify themselves by either clothes or body markings, the Mungiki have opted for a symbol more representative of their ideals – each member carries a severed human head on a spear.

DEAD

Los Angeles itself has had to endure a rising menace with the emergence of the 18th Street Gang, who consider the Bloods and the Crips both ripe for elimination.

LAPD believe that on average someone is assaulted violently by an 18th Street Gang member every single day, as they rack up a kill-count three times as high as their currently larger rivals.

Mexico is also home to powerful competing operations.

The Sinaloa Cartel is run by 'El Chapo' Guzmán, the billionaire considered one of the richest men in the world.

El Chapo means 'Shorty' in Spanish, and though diminutive in stature he has remained the most powerful drug trafficker anywhere on the globe.

50,000 lives have been lost in their battles with the equally dangerous Los Zetas, as Mexico's cities became battlegrounds for control of the drug routes to the U.S.

Loz Zetas employed Mexico's most prolific assassin, María Jiménez, aka La Tosca.

Still only 26, she was finally caught by the authorities, and confessed to murdering 20 people and numerous kidnappings.

She was paid $1,700 a month for her services.

I imagine she is fairly relaxed about her future.

Hours after her capture, 14 human heads were found inside coolers placed on the doorstep of City Hall, along with a threatening note.

Most locals believe her stay in prison will be an extremely short one, before she miraculously escapes, with some inside assistance from terrified prison guards.

The legendary gang of Japan, the Yakuza, remains dominant, and still requires members to cut all ties with their families – and also cut off one of their own fingers as a pledge of loyalty.

China's Triads have grown ever more powerful alongside the expansion of their nation's economic might.

The syndicate is in reality a conglomerate that has over 2.5 million members worldwide; each branch has its own customs and intense blood-soaked rituals.

The Russian mafia strikes dread among other criminal gangs because of their practice of not only killing their rivals, but also all of a rival's family members.

Their reach is global, and the FBI and CIA agree that if you conduct business in Russia, at least 20% of your profits will end up in their pockets.

The power of prison gangs has escalated along racial lines.

The Aryan Brotherhood is responsible for a quarter of all prison murders in the United States.

You can only become a member by killing or severely wounding fellow prisoners; this practice is known as 'blood in, blood out' – a reminder that anyone who attempts to leave the gang

DEAD

will end up dead or hospitalised and crippled.

It is difficult to know which is safer – the streets of downtown Los Angeles, a visit to Juarez in Mexico, or life inside a maximum security prison in America.

It is certainly the case that our own home-grown contenders as criminal overlords, the Kray Gang, seem genteelly British and sportsmanlike in their business dealings.

THE MAN WHO SAVED MORE LIVES THAN HITLER, STALIN, AND MAO KILLED.

ACCORDING TO THE UN, NORMAN BORLAUG IS officially 'the man who saved a billion lives'.

He developed a strain of wheat that grew faster, and cheaper, in unaccommodating terrain; it eradicated the famines caused by population expansion that began to sweep Mexico, the Middle East, and Asia in the 1960s.

Karl Landsteiner, who discovered the difference in human blood types, made possible the surgeries we now take for granted, paving the way for blood banks that save many millions of lives each year.

Edward Jenner developed the smallpox vaccine, another bewilderingly invaluable advance that saved approaching a billion lives.

Fritz Haber was a German chemist who won a Nobel Prize in 1918 for his 'Haber Process' which created synthetic fertilizers. This was at a time when most of Germany was starving, enabling many citizens to be fed from very little. His work was nicknamed 'bread from the air'.

Today, the food base for half the world's population is still grown thanks to Haber's invention. The number of lives he has saved is inestimable.

But few will know the names of these remarkable scientists, compared to the great celebrity mass killers of the 20th century.

Adolf Hitler was responsible for thirty million deaths, and Joseph Stalin's tally was about forty million.

China's Mao Zedong was the unsurpassed murderer in world history, during his 'Great Leap Forward'. Starting in the late 1950s, he simply starved his people to death, his victims numbering sixty million.

He used famine as a weapon even more effectively than Stalin.

These three charismatic leaders make other murderous tyrants appear quite kindly in comparison.

Pol Pot killed only 1.7 million of his political opponents in Cambodia in the 1970s, and Kim Il-Sung of North Korea killed merely 1.6 million of his.

Other psychopathic heads of state like Mengistu of Ethiopa, Gowon of Nigeria, Kambanda in Rwanda, Sukarno in Indonesia, all remain imprinted on our minds more deeply than billion-life-saving Norman Borlaug.

Is it the human condition that monsters are more memorable than Nobel Prize winners? Their names are certainly more easily recalled than those of people who dedicated themselves to saving lives; more lives than were ended by all the worst despots combined.

A man who rescued the lives of thousands, but is largely

forgotten today, was Pheidippides. Despite inspiring whole populations with his legendary feat, Pheidippides was an Athenian runner during the first Persian invasion of Greece in 490BC.

Before the Battle of Marathon, he was sent as a courier from Athens to Sparta to ask them for their assistance in the battle.

He ran the whole way non-stop, sprinting 140 miles and arriving the day after he left. He delivered his message, and promptly died from exhaustion on the spot.

The Spartans were able to join the Athenians at Marathon, and prevent the Persians invasion, saving the lives of all who would have died at their hands, and, arguably, the whole of Greece.

In the late 19th century when the notion for a modern Olympics was being debated, the games' creators looked to the tale of Pheidippides, himself the first true marathon runner.

They named the long distance running event The Marathon and it has featured in the Olympic Games since its inception in 1896.

Many countries around the world started organising their own Marathon style events. The length set for the run was just over 26 miles, the approximate distance from Marathon to Athens.

Obviously far shorter than Pheidippides' rather more taxing journey, it at least guaranteed fewer fatal casualties.

More recently another individual ran hundreds of miles to save his city, this time on four legs.

In 1925, a diphtheria outbreak was poised to attack the city of Nome in Northern Alaska, its most populous area at the time.

When the city doctor diagnosed a boy with tonsillitis and he died the next day, he didn't consider diphtheria; nobody else was displaying symptoms. However throughout the next

months there arose an escalating number of tonsillitis victims, and the death toll rose quickly among the city's children.

Despite its size, Nome had only one doctor, four nurses, a 24 bed hospital, and a stock of diphtheria antitoxin that had expired in 1918.

The new serum had not arrived in time, before Nome's port was frozen over as usual during the winter months.

Now only accessible by the Iditarod Trail, the primary source of mail and necessities, they could only be delivered by dog sled.

The number of citizens threatened in the affected area was around 10,000, with an almost 100% mortality rate.

Native Alaskans were being the hardest hit, with no immunity to foreign diseases.

Desperately the doctor sent a radio telegram for help: "An epidemic of diphtheria is almost inevitable here. I am in urgent need of one million units of antitoxin."

The serum that could stop the outbreak was in Anchorage, nearly a thousand miles away from Nome.

The only aircraft in the vicinity was incapacitated with a frozen engine, and wouldn't start.

The agreed that an option was a dog sled relay in the -31 degree Celsius blizzards, six hundred and seventy four treacherous miles across icy tundra. Twenty mushers, the sled drivers, took part, selecting the best dogs to haul them. Balto was one of those chosen. He ran the longest and most hazardous stretch of the run, in whiteout conditions.

The musher could barely see his hand in front of his face, but Balto somehow managed to stay on the track.

At the last stop, where their task was to be relayed over to the next in the chain, they found the final musher very soundly asleep, and in no condition to fulfil the final hurdle.

They decided they had to simply carry on, and as news of their heroism spread, when they pulled into Nome both sledder and Balto were instant celebrities.

They had made the journey in five days, saving many from death, and halting the disease from spreading further.

In New York's Central Park you will find a statue of Balto on the main path by the Children's Zoo.

PREMATVRE DEATH BY PREMATVRE OBITVARY.

MARCUS GARVEY DIED UPON SEEING HIS own obituary, printed inadvertently, in the *Chicago Defender* newspaper.

It clearly made such distressing reading for Mr Garvey, describing him as 'broke, alone, and unpopular', that he promptly dropped dead on the spot from a massive stroke. The newspaper must have congratulated itself on something of a scoop – not only breaking the news of his death first, but simultaneously causing it.

Poor George Soros, the far-from-poor billionaire financier was also distressed to read his own less than flattering obituary published by Reuters in April 2013. Reuters withdrew the story, apologising to Soros and made a statement regretting "erroneously publishing the obituary, and that Soros was alive and well".

In media circles, where forward planning is to be expected, it is standard practice to have obituaries written before the deaths of prominent people. It is more unusual to publish one.

However, it is not altogether uncommon.

Der Spiegel, the leading German magazine, mistakenly

published a draft obituary for ex-U.S. President George Bush in December 2012.

The CNN Incident of April 2003 became legendary, because of the mash-up of obituaries they accidentally placed on their online pages.

When the pre-written draft memorials for several world figures appeared, it was apparent that templates for their obituaries had been clustered together.

Queen Elizabeth the Queen Mother's memorial was muddled into the Pope's, with his "love of horse racing". Fidel Castro's obituary had taken on aspects of Ronald Reagan's – Castro was "a lifeguard, athlete, and movie star".

Although the Queen Mother was already dead, in an earlier gaffe she had already received a premature obituary of her own.

In CNN's confusion, Bob Hope's obituary told us he was the UKs favourite grandmother. He died three months later. A CNN tribute also had to be quietly removed because the subject was still alive: Nelson Mandela.

Among the 'living dead' in the music world, whose demise has been reported on various TV and radio programmes, are Madonna, (on a BBC News video) and Lou Reed (across many U.S. radio stations following a hoax Reuters email).

Vuk Peric was a Serbian pensioner who enjoyed a hoax. He placed his own death notice in a newspaper in 1997 to see who would turn up at his funeral. After watching the ceremony from a distance, he appeared and thanked everyone for attending.

Rather more bizarrely, in 2006 Alison Matera told fellow church choir members in Florida that she had cancer, and over the course of the next year gave them reports on her treatment. She finally revealed that she was close to death and was entering a hospice. In subsequent follow-up calls she masqueraded as a hospice nurse reporting to Alison's friends on her desperate condition. Finally, pretending to be her sister, she told all the choir members that poor Alison had died.

The church arranged a memorial service, to which Ms Matera showed up, hair styled and dyed differently, purporting to be her sister. But suspicions had already been aroused by the similarity of the voices of the hospice nurse and sister – they both sounded exactly like Alison Matera.

She was not arrested or charged as no crime had been committed. She blamed her preoccupation with her own death on lingering childhood traumas.

My favourite premature death report was Rudyard Kipling's, who read of his death announced in a magazine.

He wrote to the editor "I've just read that I am dead. Don't forget to delete me from your list of subscribers."

WOULD YOU CARE TO·STAR·IN A SNUFF MOVIE?

THIS WOULD NOT BE A 17TH CENTURY costume drama, filled with refined aristocrats routinely taking a pinch of scented or flavoured tobacco powder to place inside their nostrils.

Though almost none of us have ever seen a snuff movie, we know that the leading protagonist is executed live on film, the blood is authentic, and the death is genuine.

There is no great shortage of people wanting the leading role, in reality committing suicide as the murdered victim in the production.

This genre of movie making is popular in South America, and for S&M specialists they represent highly regarded entertainment.

However, in over 40 years of speculation, no real examples of snuff films have ever surfaced in the wider public realm.

In 1980 the film *Cannibal Holocaust* was released, about a group of film makers who visit an indigenous cannibalistic tribe in deepest Colombia, and mysteriously go missing.

234   DEAD

The film takes a documentary stance, decades before *The Blair Witch Project* emerged, presenting the events as reality, following a rescue team search for their disappeared co-stars.

The final scene is shot on shaky, handheld cameras by the actors themselves, and shows their ritualistic deaths at the hands of the terrifying cannibals, involving gang rape, decapitation, and butchering.

The film's most shocking moment is when the crew stumble upon the body of a girl with an upright stake impaling her body from rear end to mouth.

Her corpse is suspended halfway up, and covered in blood.

Horrified audiences were so convinced by the footage of the girl and the murdered crew they believed what they were seeing had to be real deaths.

As the movie was so clearly low budget, it seemed that the special effects to produce such realistic amputations and decapitations were unlikely; these grisly scenes simply had to be authentic.

This was confirmed when the four main actors who had died on set disappeared after filming.

The film's director, Italian Ruggero Deodato, was interrogated and finally arrested for quadruple murder.

Just as it appeared that the world had witnessed the first openly and publicly screened snuff movie, the four actors resurfaced, and went on television.

They stated that Deodato was so keen to fuel the deathly rumours, that the four had all signed contracts to disappear for a year after filming.

The fascination about snuff films started some years earlier with the Manson Family killings in 1969.

Allegedly they filmed their entire bloody rampage but the footage has never been recovered, or released.

This enigmatic taboo was coupled with a time when people were beginning to have wider access to film cameras, and undoubtedly birthed this macabre genre.

Quickly after the Manson killings, a very low cost slasher film was made called *Slaughter*, depicting a group of young, female hippies who go on a killing spree.

Shot in Argentina due to lack of funds it is mainly silent, apart from screams, as the girls couldn't speak English.

Director Allan Shackleton shelved the film, but later decided to give it an extra scene and added twist, contributing heavily to the snowballing urban legend of snuff.

Shackleton's new edit shows the cameras pulling away from the scene to film the lead actress, director and film crew on the set.

The director then advances slowly towards the actress before suddenly murdering her, watched by the rest of the crew.

He released his new filmed as *Snuff*, with the tagline 'The picture they said could never be shown! The film that could only be made in South America where life is cheap!'

Protestors immediately expressed outrage, convinced they witnessed the filming of a human death, until Shackleton made his charade finally public.

A swamp of films followed that fooled the public into thinking they were watching a snuff movie.

Faces of Death seen in 1978 was purportedly a compilation of real news reportage of deaths that were deemed too awful for television and cinema broadcast.

Well-edited around scripted material, it included suicides, accidents, and a rather convincing death by electric chair complete with foaming mouth and bleeding eyeballs.

Flower of Flesh and Blood arrived from Japan in the mid 1980s, and was so gruesome the filmmakers had to produce a

236   DEAD

'making of' video to show how it was achieved.

However, it provided the snuff hungry Japanese market something more dreadful than the American products, tragically even inspiring a genuinely brutal serial killer who terrorised Tokyo.

"Snuff is like the holy grail, much talked about, long sought after, but never yet fully confirmed." reported the FBI.

Many murderers record their conquests for personal pleasure, but the idea of releasing something into circulation and for a profit is what defines the genre.

Ted McIlvenny, is the caretaker of the world's largest sex movie archive as the director of the Institute for the Advanced Study of Human Sexuality, with a holding of 390,000 films.

He claims that in his 25 years of following porn he's seen only three films in which someone has died on camera.

One was a religious anomaly from Morocco involving a boy being torn apart by wild horses, another in which the actor died of a heart attack during an S&M scene, and one where the actor strangled himself during autoerotic asphyxiation.

With the advancement of the internet the possibility of making and also sharing snuff has increased greatly.

In Dnepropetrovsk, Ukraine in Summer 2007 two teenagers, known as the Dnepropetrovsk Maniacs, took off on a mad butchering binge, targeting vulnerable people – elderly, unwell, young, or drunk – killing them, usually with a hammer, pawning their belongings, and filming everything.

The two boys Victor Sayenko and Igor Suprunyuck both got life imprisonment for their hideous 21 murders.

As well as filming, they enjoyed sharing photos of themselves attending their victim's funerals, looking anything but sombre, fooling around and making lewd hand gestures at coffins.

When one of their films appeared on the internet, entitled *3*

DEAD

guys, 1 hammer, their little movie went viral immediately.

Clips are still available in some darker corners of the Internet, but reading reviews by the hardiest gore web trawlers are enough to stop most people in their tracks from clicking 'watch'.

This film also inspired a psychopathic killer, Luka Magnotta, a Canadian male escort and porn actor.

Magnotta was obsessed with finding fame, auditioning for a multitude of reality television shows, looking for his big break.

His intense narcissism led him to have numerous cosmetic surgeries, but he failed to make it in TV or as a successful model.

It seemed he was going to have to try another route on his pathological search for attention.

He developed a growing fixation with serial killers and the kind of admiration they attain from fans online.

His next step was to gain notoriety by torturing fluffy baby kittens – releasing two videos on various gore websites of him killing them, firstly with a vacuum cleaner, secondly fed to a large python.

Animal rights activists found the films and immediately set about trying to track the killer down.

Their searches were relentless, with Magnotta's endless aliases sending them in circles, and fears that he might hurt a child next being ignored by the police.

But Magnotta then announced "Next time you hear from me, it will be in a movie I'm producing that will have some humans in it, not just pussies."

He started promoting a new film he was working on entitled *1 lunatic, 1 icepick*, and building momentum with comments and shares through various sites.

The video was finally uploaded on to BestGore.com, and featured 11 minutes of the disturbing murder and cannibalism of Lin Jun, a Chinese exchange student at Montreal University.

Police finally took note, tracked Magnotta down and raided his blood-stained apartment.

He was already gone.

Magnotta then started releasing body parts to authorities in Canada.

He was finally found after a week in a Berlin internet café, looking at himself on the news coverage of the manhunt,

He is awaiting trial in 2014.

Would he have killed if not for the guaranteed audience in the hundreds of thousands?

BestGore and other websites are set up to show the videos banned by conventional video sharing sites like YouTube and Vimeo, and shamefully it is still legal to watch them, even the worst of the true-death offerings.

†

Note: The secret of *Cannibal Holocaust*'s stake girl? Deodato was forced to reveal his technique to prove his innocence.

The actress sat on middle of the stake on a concealed bicycle seat holding a piece of light weight wood in her mouth to indicate her teeth were removed.

Sat bolt upright, and covered in animal blood, she didn't move a muscle throughout her scene, startling audiences with a simple crudeness that a Hollywood blockbuster budget probably couldn't have created as disturbingly.

DEAD   241

SOME LIVES LEAVE A MARK. OTHERS LEAVE A STAIN.

ALMOST EVERYBODY LIVES A LIFE OF LITTLE
CONSEQUENCE TO MANKIND.
BUT WOULDN'T YOU PREFER TO HAVE SPENT
YOUR YEARS RATHER USELESSLY,
BUT ENTERTAININGLY – EVEN IF YOUR EXISTENCE
DIDN'T ACHIEVE ANYTHING MEMORABLY
SIGNIFICANT AT ALL?

DEAD

DEAD

Charles Saatchi founded the global advertising agency Saatchi & Saatchi in 1970 which grew to become the largest agency in the world. At the same time Saatchi began collecting art and later opened his first gallery a 30,000 square foot ex-paint factory in Boundary Road, London. His exhibitions have always focused on contemporary artists and Saatchi's *Sensation* exhibition of Young British Artists in 1997 at the Royal Academy, London and at the Brooklyn Museum of Art, New York sparked an explosion of controversy.

Saatchi has been one of the moving forces of the modern age, vigorously shaping the contemporary art world, and was selected by the BBC as one of 60 'New Elizabethans' who has most influenced the past 60 years.

The 70,000 square foot Saatchi Gallery in the Duke of York's HQ King's Road is one of the largest showcases of contemporary art in the world. It has hosted fifteen of the twenty most visited exhibitions in London over the last 5 years in the Art Newspaper annual museum visitor surveys and is amongst the top five most popular museums in the world on Facebook, and Twitter, and Google+.

Saatchi's previous books include The *Naked Eye* which featured remarkable unphotoshopped images, *Babble, Be The Worst You Can Be*, and his first book *My Name Is Charles Saatchi and I'm an Artoholic* in which he answered questions from journalists, critics, and members of the public with brutally frank candour.

First published 2015
Booth-Clibborn Editions
Editorial Director: Katherine Hawker
Editorial Associates: Natasha Hoare and Holly Parkhouse
Design by Sean Murphy
Text copyright © Charles Saatchi, 2015
Book copyright © Booth-Clibborn Editions, 2015
Author photograph by James King

Booth-Clibborn Editions
Studio 83, 235 Earl's Court Road
London SW5 9FE
info@booth-clibborn.com
www.booth-clibborn.com

Printed and bound in China

ISBN 978-1-86154-359-2